To Jo

My
Moments in Time

Bailey

MW00790584

Death by Silence

GLENWOOD BURLEY

Author
Glenwood Burley - HawkCode587@gmail.com

Burley Hollow
PO Box 3494
Richmond, VA 23235

Cover Design - Matthew Stinnett

Graphic design - Dianne C. Dementi

Publisher
Wayne Dementi
Dementi Milestone Publishing, Inc.
Manakin-Sabot, VA 23103
www.dementimilestonepublishing.com

Library of Congress Control Number: 2020921278

ISBN: 978-1-7350611-9-1

Printed in the USA   First Edition

TABLE OF CONTENTS

ACKNOWLEDGMENTS

Katie Dunn
Grammar Coach

Margaret Kostal
Manuscript Consultant

Pegi Einig – Robin Beres – Penn Burke
Di Birchak – Patse Younkins
Shelia Maynus – Matthew Stinnett – Susan Dunn

In Memory

Ernest Bentley Burley

&

Aileen Elizabeth Copper Burley

INSPIRATIONAL

Chief Alfred Durham

H. Penn Burke

Terelle Robinson

Agent Ed Sulzbach, Jr.

Nancy Thomas

Adrian Clark

Claude "CL" Moore

Thomas A. Silvestri

Stuart R. Kaplan

Jim Crotty

Hope Platt

Robert J. Arnold, Ed. D.

*"No matter the mountain's height,
nor the ocean's depth, the power of faith
is the foremost component of my success
and well-being.
To have reached that pinnacle,
and stood upon the cornerstone of Jesus Christ
—
is a milestone of my time"*

Glenwood Ware Burley

PREFACE

The sound of silence is a cry in the night screaming for love — and there is none. Sounds of emptiness linger like a morning fog, stealing my belonging. Nearby orchards of reds, oranges and golden tans, backyard mountains strutting their colors like bold peacocks, and the ever cooling breeze are mere boyhood memories. Nature's beauty embraces me at dawn, to the sound of a distance cowbell. Burley Hollow is home — not knowing any difference beyond.

The takeaway from this journey is that I received a second chance – twice!

First, my intent and plans to commit suicide were intercepted by immediate psychiatric hospitalization. Second, was proudly becoming a better Father! Learning from my mistakes and yesterday's failures provided a foundation to change and live a better life. With a destiny to live — I became a better man.

Humans die every day on this Earth, not knowing who they really are. Some live six to nine decades, never knowing or understanding how or why they think as they do! Their rooms of darkness – the evils of hate, hurt, and rejection fester in their souls throughout life. Sadly, they decay from within. Years of childhood darkness, two decades of law enforcement, compounded with overwhelming medical challenges disintegrated my will to live.

The roadblock to this madness of destructive crash and burn was confinement and intense therapy at the Medical College of Virginia Hospital, in Richmond. (VCU Health Systems). Six weeks in psychiatry was the greatest blessing received that gave me a new day, and beyond. With a hospital support team, and my commitment to conquer a productive quality of life, sunshine prevailed and demons vanished. A cornerstone of healing was built that took me to levels during the last half of my life far reaching in terms of contributions and achievements!

Give **Death by Silence** to someone that is tailspinning and struggling to level their wings to a successful flight in life. Hand this book to a friend that is flaming in hatred, spitting scorn upon all who suffer from it. Help heal a sad child that you once knew, now grown. Reading this book may help that person learn to forgive, accept yesterday. and find peace.

Hug someone! If they are special — tell them you love them.

Life was given a new day — I am forever thankful.

Defining Moment

It was the winter of 1985, a few days before Christmas, and for me time had frozen. The arctic winds cut at my face as they blew across the noisy rapids of the nearby James River. Flowing through the capital city of Richmond, Virginia, it allowed the vortex winds to swirl full force through the streets and alleys.

I stood alone at 12th and Broad Street that frigid morning, near the Medical College of Virginia Hospital, currently the VCU Medical Center. I had been at this intersection thousands of times, walking my beat as a rookie policeman or driving to and from my patrol assignment in Fulton Bottom. During my tour I frequently responded to the MCV emergency rooms, investigating and taking police reports of homicides, rapes, and a variety of assaults.

This morning was different. My surroundings felt intimidating. I felt vulnerable, frightened, and alone. Dressed in street clothes, I was without a badge and gun. There was no wife or family member at my side, and no home to which I could return. Moments earlier, the Psychiatric unit on West 7 had released me from a six-week hospitalization including two weeks in intensive care. The reality of this moment heightened my fears of uncertainty. My challenges in life had been psychologically and medically devastating. The path to my future would be mine to walk, providing me visions of a new day. Awareness and acceptance that I no longer was Officer Glenwood Burley, just Glen Burley — was a defining moment.

I came to West 7 physically weak, malnourished, and dehydrated. I was severely depressed, totally withdrawn from reality, and intentions to commit suicide. My physical and mental stability were at their lowest points. I had mastered a technique of denial and disguise over the years. My portrayal of smiles and congeniality camouflaged my emptiness. However, my condition was so critical that this technique was no longer effective. My inability to function and my dire need of professional intervention prompted my wife Gwen to contact Captain Charles "Chuck" Bennett, a very special friend to both of us. I held high admiration for Chuck and Gwen hoped I would accept his advice. Captain Bennett had knowledge of my tailspin and understood her desperation for help.

I heard Chuck's voice in the kitchen. The sunset had succumbed to darkness. I felt a hand on my shoulder moments later. Chuck had found me slumped over at the dining room table. He witnessed my facial emptiness as the candle light flickered its dancing reflections across a room of darkness, silence, and sadness. He helped me stand, and embraced me. Gwen was nowhere to be seen. Chuck told me he loved me and how important it was for me to get well. He continued by saying how extremely proud he was of me. He had been my South side precinct captain for several years. It was an effort for me to remain standing as I broke into an emotional collapse. The silence was deep. He paused for a moment longer and said, "We need to take a little ride downtown." He blew out the candle — I knew it was time to go.

When Captain Bennett transported me to the hospital, I accepted admission to the psychiatric unit in lieu of a mental process (green warrant) being filed prior to my admission. It was a silent stipulation to the judicial procedure that I was unquestionably in need of professional help and protection from self harm. This little ride downtown and admission to West 7 were long overdue!

MCV's Department of Psychology provided me with the best of intensive counseling. It was a unique position for me as a mental patient. I was known as a police officer throughout the metropolitan community. The Richmond News Leader ran a front page top-fold article about me the day of my retirement eight days earlier. Most notably, my wife, a registered nurse, held an administrative position at the very same hospital. I was assigned a five-member team, who quickly evaluated my patient profile. Their first objective was to target my specific dysfunctional traits. From the initial shock of confinement, to the day of my release, the hospital's professional services were superb.

Health improvements were evident in the early weeks of hospitalization. Several days of nutritional meals enhanced my body stamina. I opted to use the solitary confinement room with padded walls and floor to run in place and build up core body strength. Once I became nutritionally stabilized and had several nights of decent sleep with medication, specialists were eager to pick my brain.

No one cut me any slack. A suicidal policeman in a mental unit married to an administrative nurse whose office was several floors below created a buzz of employee gossip. My team quickly established issues that were haunting my past and placed them directly on the table for discussion. I initially attempted to skirt the big ones by dancing around them, however, I quickly learned that dancing with them wasn't an option.

Eight days earlier, before my hospitalization, I hosted a farewell breakfast in the police headquarters cafeteria. On the surface, it was planned as a farewell retirement breakfast to thank those in attendance. My masterful trait of disguise was working its magic. I had invited city officials, judges, lawyers, the police chief and his command staff. After our meal everyone sat in silence, including my wife who was holding our two-year-old son, Nicholas.

No one knew that days earlier I had walked from my home to the nearby James. Surrounded by the roaring rapids, I sat on a boulder and wrote a suicidal goodbye speech. Showing no evidence of despair or despondence I stood tall that morning smiling with pride and humble appreciation as I read that note to all in attendance for the respect and support everyone had given to me.

That morning and up to midnight, there would be no tricks or treats for me and my family. It was Halloween, October 31st 1985, my last day in that beautiful blue uniform, serving twenty-one plus years with the Richmond Bureau of Police. I continued to wear my uniform long after the ceremony and up until bedtime.

Gwen unexpectedly came home that afternoon to check on me. Not aware I was still in uniform, she took out her Canon AE-1 and took some pictures of me in the front yard. My badge was my life. Being a police officer was my passion and identity. Aside from when my father died in 1971, this day in Richmond was indeed, my darkest and most defining moment.

A significant turning point in my career came in the early months of that year. It would be my last tour in my patrol unit. It was a day shift and the morning sun was reaching for noon. I drove behind the Stony Point Shopping Center and parked. The reality of my surroundings was an indescribable black hole. The battles were over and I had lost the war. My spirit had died. My focus and the ability to properly patrol the streets had realistically vanished, overwhelming my sense of adequacy.

Sergeant Burt Walker, the Police Bureau Risk Management Officer was notified. In minutes he arrived and immediately assessed my mental state. Only three hours into my shift, I was marking out of service, turning off the radio, and locking the police unit. Sgt. Walker helped transfer my attaché case and jacket to his unit.

The Police administration had been monitoring my declining health and questionable ability to remain on patrol for some months. We rode in silence traveling down Forest Hill Avenue as he took me home. There was nothing to say. I remember the awkwardness as I sobbed uncontrollably. Walkers' priorities were my safety, the safety of the public, and of the fellow officers, with whom I worked.

Medical disability papers were filed in April, which started the process toward my retirement. My 43rd birthday came in August. I had nothing to celebrate because every moment I was in the throes of depression. The ever-lingering awareness that my days on the street were numbered produced an internal restlessness and apprehension of departure that were nipping at my heart and soul.

It was mid September when I learned my retirement date. My masterful ability to project a cool and calm demeanor was shattered by this new reality. The decline of my mental stability had begun. The internal quandary was beginning to fester, causing a turbulence in my mind and creating a tailspin of dark despair and self destruction.

Miles from Nowhere

Dirty fingernails, poor dental hygiene, and scarcely a heartbeat for education — these were my childhood norms growing up in rural western Amherst County, Virginia. Our low income farming families faced untold challenges associated with two World Wars and the Korean War. Many of the men went overseas to fight.

By the time I was eight, I knew the drill. At the break of dawn, my Dad walked down the hallway and stood at the base of the stairway. The aroma of fresh coffee, and fried country ham signaled the four-word command was next: "Time to get up!" He shouted out, with clarity and firmness, setting the tone for the day. He gave no thought that I was a little boy, tucked snugly in my straw bed, yet without hesitation his command was honored.

I'm 77 now, and as I reflect back to the 1940s and 1950s on Burley Hollow, I would best describe the families in that community, as self sustaining proud people — who were meek, honorable and poor, yet rich in integrity and credibility. Conversationalists, they were not. We shared the feelings of being blessed by the natural surroundings, rich soil, and crisp spring water. Traditionally, Sunday was revered as the Lord's day.

As a child, having cousins aplenty, the "hollow" was our community. The darkest of nights, the nearby hugging mountains, and the haunting quietness instilled an emptiness in me. Heavy fog played magic before daylight and concealed the fruit orchards. Vibrant rays of the morning sun brought my blessings back in to focus – its power and warmth glowed upon row after row of blooming peach trees, signaling spring had arrived.

The hollow had many paths zigzagging across hay fields and mountain slopes. My most popular path had an oak foot log spanning across a creek. Some twenty feet long it was worn flat from decades of foot traffic. This path led up to two homes on the mountain's edge. That huge log was my partner, as it enabled me to climb that ridge and charm my three aunts for some homemade cake, pie, or cookies. I never cared which sweets my aunts Ora, Ruth or Ruby baked, because every bite was scrumptious!

By chance, if I had a quarter burning my pocket, it was no effort to walk two miles out to Sardis' store for a moon pie and a Coke. Sardis Grocery, with two gas pumps – one regular, one high octane -- was a community lifeline selling basic essentials. Dad never filled the gas tank on his 1946 Chevy pickup -- he always pumped the same "dollar and a half," providing about six gallons, which lasted for months.

A visit to my Mom's family demanded a vehicle. Her relatives lived twenty miles due west in Buena Vista. The trip involved a winding, highway across the Blue Ridge Mountains and then a curvy decent into the sleepy village. Seven miles east of Burley Hollow was the little town of Amherst, always luring with candy and toys at the "dime store." It seemed like — I was miles from nowhere!

The silence of the nights, except for an occasional bobcat scream, left me with a sense of disconnection and loneliness. The nights seemed to last forever. Dad always "went to bed with the chickens." Like clockwork, he rose before daylight when the chief rooster performed his traditional morning crow. Because I was of three children, my Mom seemed to be more attentive to my two younger siblings, Sam and Becky, than she was to me. Our household did not seem to have an embracing atmosphere; thus saplings of questionable self worth and low esteem took root.

I was indoctrinated into the farming culture from a young age, receiving no encouragement to venture beyond the sunrise and lifestyle of Burley Hollow. A silent assumption was that I would, like my father and grandfather, remain true to our traditional toil of the farmland; feeding our families, praising our God, and being honorable Burleys.

In retrospect, education wasn't criticized in any regard. It simply wasn't endorsed in my household as a key element to a progressive or successful adulthood. Actually more emphasis was placed on immediately removing your school clothes upon arriving home and replacing them with "work clothes." After a snack of corn bread mixed in a glass of cold buttermilk, I was good to go! Homework wasn't a priority. It followed gathering firewood, filling wood boxes, and then feeding the hogs. With suppertime near, I finished my least appealing task – hurrying to the barn, to feed and milk two cows!

Farming blessed me with so much experience of nature, crop growing, and raising and selling pigs. Learning the land and knowing how to acquire the highest growth productivity were priceless. Farming taught me lessons to be appreciative. It simplified my closeness to life and gratitude for food, as well as grounding me with the beauty of existence.

My parents and teachers did not take the time to evaluate my potential as a student or my overall development as a person. Both unknowingly let me slip through the cracks. I lacked academic focus and adult investment in education — perhaps I would have been a more successful student had more importance been assigned to my achievement and personal growth.

Not returning to Amherst County High School on the fourth day of my senior year was a decision I made with haste and poor judgment. Without a thought for the consequences, I simply quit. My commitment to a purpose, and self confidence toward achievement were absent. Selfishness blinded my focus to graduate with my senior class. I have my class ring, but not the memories of that commencement ceremony.

My parents never sat down with me to discuss their disappointment with my actions. In fairness to them, I gave no indication to anyone that I was quitting school. They took no actions individually or collectively, to emphasize the importance of education and acquiring my diploma. However, given what my mother and father knew or did not know, what they had, or not — they did the very best they could. I am who I am today — because of them.

Burley Hollow

Peach picking was at its peak. The United States was in the midst of World War II. There among the summer mountain breezes I became a new infant sporting homemade diapers, cut from worn bed sheets — another Burley Hollow boy!

I was born in an eight-room farm house that was my home from my diaper days until my eighteenth birthday. Little did I know a new world awaited as I eventually would join the army. From an innocent farm boy, to becoming a paratrooper was truly a leap! Those youthful eighteen years would be remembered as precious, blessed, and unforgettable. Yet, there were moments in time, sometimes only in seconds that cut away at my childhood, and darkened the sunshine of my youth.

Seven miles west of the town of Amherst lies the first evidence of elevation to the Tobacco Row Mountains. Adjacent to and towering behind them are Long Mountain, then the Blue Ridge. Driving west on US Route 60, you came upon a dirt road that took you between two small mountain ridges leading into Burley Hollow. With ruts aplenty, this road ran along a creek that formed from natural springs, far up the mountain. These springs and creeks provided water for our families.

Some three generations earlier, a Burley family from Scotland laid claim to 1400 acres of this low-line mountain area with rich farm land potential. For more than two centuries, that mile and a half muddy dirt road, now black topped, has been a gateway to the rest of Virginia and beyond. I entered this world from that road, from that mountain, and from that hollow — Burley Hollow!

The Burley traditions I experienced pretty much mirrored what took place in generations past, whereby everyone lived off the land. Farming, harvesting fruit from peach and apple orchards, planting crops and gardens, raising hay to feed the cattle, and growing tobacco were templates for survival. We sold young calves for veal. For hundreds of years we killed hogs on Thanksgiving Day regardless of weather or temperature. Some families killed a heifer in the fall. The beef menu was an occasional treat for the daily pork lovers. Chickens and fresh eggs were as essential as dry firewood from the woodpile stacked neatly on the back porch. Everyone cooked and heated their homes with firewood. Many times, mom sent me to the henhouse to gather fresh laid eggs for making pies and cakes. I liked that chore because I knew sweets were not a daily delight. Of course, all hen houses had a rooster or two!

My families essentially lived off the land and were blessed with rich bottom soil that provided top quality produce. The spring water was always ice cold. Our spring was above our house, so we could pipe gravity fed water directly into the kitchen. Until I was tall enough, around the age of ten, my mom kept a step stool under the sink. Whenever I became thirsty, I would drag out the stool, and stand on it to reach the handmade aluminum dipper hanging on a nail.

Our hot water heater was our Home Comfort cook stove. It had a twenty-gallon water tank mounted inside the frame to the right of the oven. Mom cooked three meals daily, so we always had warm water. If we needed hot water, she just placed some on the top over the wood fire! Mom's kitchen lured me as it was always cozy, with a little trail of steam escaping from the stove top kettle. My little brain was always searching for freshly made goodies in her "office."

The Burleys and the women who married into the family had established reputations as excellent cooks. All the printed cook books in the hollow wouldn't fill a large Ziploc bag. Mom and my aunts all cooked from memory and by taste. I never remember seeing a measuring cup. Mom would say, "I used a tad of this" or "a pinch of that." Her best recipes? No, don't ask — she would never reveal her secrets. No way!

The water ran directly from a mountain spring some three hundred yards above the house. There was no faucet, so it ran constantly. How many dippers? Only one – yes, and used by everyone. If "Uncle Hal" or Andrew Floyd visited, well they would grab the same dipper, and take a swig!

Summertime was demanding on the farm. Harvesting our apples and peaches called for all hands on deck. My cousins and I were the water bucket runners. Playfully swinging a small metal bucket with the dipper clanging inside, our water source was not from the house, which was too far away. Depending on our location, the nearest spring or creek would suffice to quench everyone's thirst.

Our spring did double duty. Water ran into the kitchen sink, and continued some fifteen feet outside into a spring house. This little building near the back door had a cement reservoir inside designed to hold water at the depth of ten inches. This allowed us to store milk, keeping it cool for weekly pickup by the milk company.

The milkman came early at the break of dawn. Dad hauled the steel cans of milk down to the road on my wooden wagon. The driver loaded our fresh milk into his refrigerated truck and left us last week's empty cans. The ever-flowing water through the spring house was a cost-efficient cooling system.

As I write this, an afterthought comes to mind. Our hog pen was below and off to the side of our house. Why didn't we run pipe from the spring house to the hog pen? It would have saved everyone many steps and lots of energy during the hot summer months lugging water to the hog trough. Some fifty years later and I think of this.

Burley Hollow was full of life. Every day was a daylight to dark endeavor with continued duties and responsibilities. Farming is a demanding and dependant enterprise. All of our cattle, hogs, chickens, the living fruit trees and vegetables depended on us to feed, cultivate and harvest them. We each had a role in contributing to that goal.

It would be accurate to describe my Burley Hollow relatives as men who ran the farms, and women, who cooked, fed, clothed the family and attended to the children. A partnership role in farm life was vital. Farming can be unpredictable and create challenges, and sometimes stress everyone.

One hot humid summer day, lightening struck a large popular tree that was on a fence line. The powerful electrical bolt traveled downward, splintering the tree trunk, and jumping onto the wire fence. It continued onto twelve beautiful Black Angus cattle sheltering in the shade, killing them all. This was a major loss for my family.

Someone forgot a sunset ritual — to close the hen house door. The next morning revealed a price for that mistake. There were dead chickens aplenty in the henhouse and throughout the back yard. The Red fox and hawk were known to strike at weak moments. Roaming dogs nearby could never be trusted either.

My Burley relatives were rich in a silent pride of being Burleys. Our name represented honesty, respect, character, and our commitment was evident every Sunday as we attended Sardis Methodist Church. We religiously honored the seventh day as the Lord's day, a day of rest. The only exception was if we had cured hay lying in the fields and thunderstorms seemed likely. The men and older children would hastily change out of church clothes, to gather and harvest the winter feed before it became damaged.

My dad was one of eight children. Like many of his siblings, he did not finish high school. He grew up during the World War 1 era and attended only eight years of school. Formal education was not part of my family's profile.

I learned early to do as I was told. I respected my elders, shook hands, and was expected to say "No sir" and "Yes ma'am." I was expected to be well mannered, quiet, and certainly not interruptive. I learned mostly by facial expression. Little to no discussion usually took place regarding how to do things.

When milking cows, stacking firewood, and picking fruit, all had techniques. I learned by silently watching. If I swayed from my teachings, hailed upon me were storms of profanity. My reward for doing things correctly was mere silence.

From my time of departure, even to this moment Burley Hollow beckons me. The creeks and the road are still there, yet the livelihood and heartbeat of my uncles, aunts, and relatives are gone. My home burned to the ground in February 1971. Throughout the hollow, pig pens, chicken houses, and hay barns stand empty and helpless. Collapsing now due to the winds of time and human abandonment, they are towering memories of my childhood in the farming fields of yesterday.

The mountainous tree lines have slowly encroached upon the once green and productive hay fields. Today those fields have no purpose and seem too long for Black Angus to graze. The distant sound of a cow bell is forever silent. I might find an old Winesap apple tree, planted in the 1940's, still fighting for life with one or two branches bearing a handful of fruit.

When I return to the hollow and smell the fresh mountain air swooping down across Devil's Pocket, or Punk Ridge, I am reminded of just how humble and thankful this place makes me feel. This land gave me dirty fingernails, cow manure between my toes, freedom, and special aunts. I go back, and stand where things were once, grasping memories from the elusive heartbeat of yesterday. Did I just see a Guernsey milk cow, grazing in the rich green pasture or hear a faint piglet grunt, his snout deep in dirt? Maybe not. Thoughts of times past embrace me as I scan the mountains, silently yielding a tiny smile, pushing back the emptiness — allowing the crisp air to dry my tears.

Despite the events that cut to my heart, this small tract of God's land, including my parents, relatives and this community have all blessed me with a foundation of character, honor, and the pride that travel with me to this day. My childhood memories, good and bad will forever dance in my heart and I will cherish them as unforgettable moments in time.

Burley Hollow was yesterday —

THE INNOCENCE OF TRUST

After the first paragraph of this chapter — stop! Place my book on your lap, pause and reflect for a moment. How recently have you witnessed a child walking alone down a road? When have you answered the front door, surprised to be greeted by a ten-year-old boy carrying a box, selling twenty-five varieties of flower seed? He has no bicycle, there is no adult with him, and no other homes are in sight.

Society has so drastically changed that our young children have become prisoners within their own neighborhoods. Today, in some parts of the United States children are not afforded the luxury of freedom and safety beyond their doorways. They are likewise overshadowed with constant observation at schools and churches. Even during an Easter egg hunt on the church lawn, parents patrol like secret service agents. Today parents are programmed to interact with their kids under the assumption that danger or abduction lurks just footsteps away. This cultural mindset steals a child's freedom of trust.

My son Nicholas was born decades after the children from my first marriage. As a retired police officer, I was aware of the criminal element, especially sexual predators, I had a delicate balancing act of not being overly protective while concealing my concern for his safety. A young child, like a pet, can perceive anxiety levels. Acting overly protective can impact a child's sense of security. I knew I couldn't catnap at an Interstate rest stop while allowing a five-year-old to scamper inside to the bathroom!

Backyard fences and cement sidewalks were not part of my youth. Approximately two acres of yard surrounded my home. Walking out the back door, I had human foot paths trailing through the grass. The main path started at the back door and split three ways — one to the hen house, one to the wood pile shed, and the third leading off down to the hog pen and Johnny house, each complimenting the other! Even today I can faintly see the indentations of years of human foot traffic. The one most traveled led to the wood pile. One Christmas I received a green toy wagon. It was all wood, designed with four vertical side slats. Its identity as a toy became questionable as I grew older. Many wagon loads of fire wood were hauled along that main path to the house. Also, it nicely accommodated two bushel baskets causing, it to be popular during harvesting seasons.

Once I walked past the wood pile, hay fields and peach orchards greeted me. Then no matter what direction I walked I was in the mountains. My next door neighbors, all aunts and uncles, lived in houses further up the mountain. From my bedroom window, when the autumn leaves fell, I could see the smoke from their chimneys. No homes were visible from our front yard. Notably, there was no foot path evident in our front yard. I walked just as much over the front as I did the back but was expected not to walk the exact same route to create a path. The front yard had a respected status and the back yard didn't. Additional structures located in front were the pickup truck shed, corn house, and hay, and stable barns.

During spring time, visitors most likely would see young piglets peeking back at them as they scampered under the barn logs. Our two work horses usually hung out near their barn stalls. They appreciated Sunday, as it was their only day off! Milk cows with chickens at their feet looking for grit, ignored new arrivals. Our beautiful Black Angus bull and his herd might have been nearby in the shade, chewing their cud.

Being surrounded daily by this domestic animal tranquility of quietness and calm created a feeling of protection for me. Our home, my bedroom, even the Johnnie House, were inside a perimeter of barns and sheds, showering me with feelings of security and trust.

I never knew restrictions or boundaries, implied or taught. Fences and gates were for the livestock. To me, this childhood environment and lifestyle established no subconscious awareness of fear and apprehensions. Oh yes, the hollow had a Boogeyman." He was Willie Burley and he lived down in the bottom on a smaller tract of land. He never owned a vehicle, and was seen often walking in the community. My older cousins talked of their fear of him. Mostly the girls seemed spooked by his nearness. The folklore was that Willie sold apple cider, but his true profit was selling corn whiskey, legally referred to as "ardent spirits." When Willie sold a case, (four one-gallon glass jugs) of cider, one jug actually contained whiskey. Of course his whiskey lovers praised how great his cider tasted.

At age five, I had firmed up my hopes and dreams of becoming a police officer in my hometown of Amherst. Another preteen aspiration was playing Major League baseball. I had visions of pitching and playing shortstop with the New York Yankees. Many boys in my school wanted to be like Mickey Mantle, Ted Williams, or Ty Cobb. Playing baseball was much higher on my dream list than milking Holstein cows!

Sports were not discussed in my home. My father despised baseball. He adamantly claimed it was a waste of time. I collected a few Topps baseball cards on occasion by buying a thin sliver of bubble gum wrapped with one card for five cents.

Adults and parents today must maintain a constant vigil over our innocent youth, as the Internet has made access to child pornography easily accessible to child molesters and abusers. In contrast, no knowledge of the evils existed in my community. The topics never came up in our homes, schools or church. My cousins and I were free spirits during our entire youth, squirrel hunting, and venturing across farmland and through wooded properties on worn paths that joined neighbors.

I have requested that when I die, my baseball glove be placed in my casket, along with a baseball pitched by my son Nick, during one of his winning Little League games. My first moments in Heaven will be finding my Father. First, I want a very long hug — a hug I've never received! Next, we'll pitch some ball, something we never have done. After we've tossed some, I will walk up to him, smile then say, "Dad, I love you." I have yearned to hear him say those very same words to me my entire life.

Despite my Father's damnation for baseball, he made one concession. At least he allowed me to play the game — well some. Getting home from practice after school or getting to a game on Saturday morning required logistics. I had to walk miles, and miles, and master the art of hitch hiking! Nope, there was no city bus, no skateboard or bicycle. Soccer moms didn't exist. I didn't dare ask anyone in the hollow to take me nine miles to practice or play baseball. Sports were about as popular as copperheads!

Saturday mornings were the ultimate moments of innocence and trust. I stood at the intersection of a gravel road leading from the hollow, and highway Route 60. More than a mile, cleats strung over my shoulder, my baseball glove in hand, I would make the journey down to the highway. The excitement of the morning far exceeded the slightest doubt that the motorist would give me a ride to Amherst.

My anticipation was high. I thought," I'm going to get to play Little League baseball today – hopefully!" Standing there in nature's silence, without a house in sight, I heard the distant sound of a vehicle descending the curves down Long Mountain. Was this driver traveling from Cincinnati to Virginia Beach, or was he a mountaineer driving down from of the Blue Ridge Mountains? Was it the church pastor, a farmer, or a felon? The car came into view, and my young heart was pounding in my chest. "Please stop!" I thought. "I don't want to miss the bus taking the team to the game in Lynchburg." I never gave one thought that I might be in harm's way!

I hitchhiked more frequently returning from the games and practice than to them. In the center of the town of Amherst was a traffic circle, one of two original circles remaining in Virginia, where US Routes 29 and 60 intersect. Homeward bound, my right thumb pointed skyward, I patiently awaited a ride again. When hitchhiking back after the game, sometime the motorist would treat me and take me all the way home. If I was let off at the highway, a long uphill trek greeted me.

I think tonight I will pray to God, thanking him for the kind motorists and many childhood blessings of protection he gave me.

The Eagle Soars

I knew immediately upon quitting high school that my mistake in doing so would impact my self-respect and emotional stability. Within months after leaving Amherst High, infatuation ruled my day. Soon after walking away from my senior class, I got married. My new bride was Edith Mae Smith, a freshman attending Brookville School near Lynchburg, Virginia. We thought we were blindly in love. Raging hormones and stupidity were flames that glowed from our passion.

The State of Virginia rejected our marriage license application. You would wonder why? Our next attempt was North Carolina. Well, we were making progress — I was old enough, but she was not, even with parental approval. Determined little love birds, we called authorities in South Carolina. Bingo! They said over the telephone, "Come on down." There was one hurdle — Edith needed to have one parent present to sign the papers that granted permission to marry and this parent was also required to attend the ceremony.

Despite our youth, immaturity, and determination, no parental opposition took place. There was no discussion whatsoever by my parents. Edith's parents seemed somewhat elated over the idea. The most startling revelation after the marriage was when Mrs. Smith informed me that my father had visited her home prior to our marriage and asked her to persuade us not to get married. Why my father never came to me — we'll never know.

It was midnight and Edith and I were ecstatic. Southbound in my 1956 Ford, we headed down Route 29 out of Lynchburg. You couldn't get a pack of chewing gum between us as her fingers tickled my right leg. Riding shotgun next to her was her mother, Mrs. Lizzie Smith. She seemed rather relaxed and ready for our all-night trek to South Carolina. When we loaded the car she tucked a little lunch bag filled with fried bologna and cheese sandwiches and a jug of sweet iced tea into the back seat.

Excited, somewhat comical, and a little sad, we were two kids dragging a parent across three states in the middle of the night to get married. The darkness of the night blinded everyone's judgment. We rolled down roads never traveled — through states we'd never seen. Love was powerful, like roaring waters. Nothing was stopping us now.

We clicked them off — Virginia and North Carolina. We battled fatigue and the sun's brightness as we pulled into York. Near Kings Mountain, York was like many South Carolinian towns — a post office and grocery store with one gas pump, and a cluster of homes along the highway. Our destination stood out. On a knoll perched above the road was a small Baptist church, white with a towering steeple. Just a few steps away sat a two-story cottage where the church pastor resided. He also served as the Justice of the Peace.

This gentleman knew we were scheduled to arrive per a telephone conversation the previous day. After hearing the gravel crackle on his parking lot, he walked out to greet us. Wearing bib overalls, jolly with smiles aglow, he welcomed us inside. He looked to be about 70. What occurred during the next ninety minutes was pleasantly unforgettable!

The first few minutes he was all business, examining everyone's legal documents to verify identity and age. Mrs. Smith signed the papers, and took an oath that she was Edith's mother. What happened next was a surprise. He extended an invitation for us to go upstairs to take showers then get dressed in our nicer clothes. He continued by informing us that he was going to make us breakfast in the meantime. Tired, hungry and needing a shower, we did not hesitate to accept his offer.

His full course breakfast was delicious. We were treated like family. Before we finished eating, he excused himself and returned wearing his pastoral attire. Because there were only three of us, we opted to take our wedding vows in his home rather than next door at the chapel. This was indeed a low maintenance ceremony — no tuxedo, gown, or flowers! The smiling Justice presented us with a certificate and said, "Mr. and Mrs. Burley congratulations! That will be $15."

Wow! A delicious meal, quick wedding vows and these two kids were finally husband and wife. Joy and anticipation swirled around us as we loaded up to return to Virginia. Obviously this adventure was a bit tiring for Mrs. Smith. She slipped into the back seat, popped off her shoes, gathered up some loose clothes for a pillow and stretched out. We made sure that we had all of our legal papers, and hadn't left any items upstairs. The Justice was genuine and kind. He seemed to enjoy every moment of our visit. Blessing us with prayer and hugs, he wished us safe travels home. We left him standing in the same place we first saw him. I still remember his smile, our laughter, and the sound of crackling gravel.

Well into Virginia, we were making good time. Earlier we stopped at Shoney's Big Boy and ordered milkshakes to drink with our remaining bologna sandwiches. The sunset was to my left as I drove north through Altavista. I had driven all night and most of the day. My new wife was not old enough to have a driver's license and her mother wasn't familiar with a stick shift, leaving me to be the sole driver.

Thirty miles to go and we would be home. The milkshakes had made us all sleepy. My car radio was blaring rock and roll, as Mrs. Smith had fallen back to sleep and Edith was lying across the front seat with her head resting on my lap. She was aware that I was fighting fatigue and squirming trying to stay awake. She started sliding her fingertips between my legs, and running her hand under my shirt to caress my chest.

My shirt was unbuttoned and I felt her lips kissing my rib cage. I experienced no difficulty staying awake now as her new territory of touch was now becoming a distraction. Somehow my left hand had ventured inside her blouse.

BAM! — A shocking silence, still, then screams! I had slammed my car into the rear of a dump truck stopped at a traffic light. The impact had thrown Edith into the floor. Mrs. Smith was thrown against the back of our front seats then dropped onto the floorboard. X-rays later revealed that she had bruised ribs and a broken wrist. The poor lady paid a heavy price for her kindness.

A Virginia State Trooper quickly arrived. Thankfully the truck driver was not injured and his truck had no damage. My vehicle was still running despite shattered headlights, and my grill and hood crushed against the radiator. No one was bleeding. I told the trooper only part of the story — that we were all tired after driving down south to get married and we were returning home. Information was exchanged and no traffic summons was issued. Rear-ending a stopped vehicle in a travel lane clearly constituted reckless driving. If the trooper had learned the total story, I would have most certainly been charged.

Two days later we waved goodbye to Mrs. Smith as she stood on her front porch. She was smiling with reserve as we departed on our honeymoon. She seemed happy for us despite having a sore rib cage and her arm slinging in a cast!

Passionate sex and small talk cannot get a person but so far in daily life. Realities were moving front and center and they were not appealing. As newlyweds, we lived in my parent's home on the second floor. Edith had been tossed into a mountainous farming zone with zero plans of a future. I started working for Mr. Richard M. Wydner Sr. owner of Amherst Milling Company as a sales representative selling flour, livestock feed, and cornmeal. This left Edith alone in Burley Hollow, without any purpose or established relationship with my parents, who allowed little time for leisurely chats. Bored and homesick, she called her mom to come get her. In months she was gone!

As a married couple our collective focus on tomorrow's path was looking dismal. Just turning fifteen, and in a short period of time she had abandoned her school, classmates, and friends. She left her lifetime neighborhood and now was missing her mother's cooking. My income from the milling company was minimum so we had no opportunity to rent an apartment. It was at this moment my childhood visions of being a policeman suddenly resurfaced. However, I was too young to join the local sheriff or town police agencies.

I visited an Army recruiting office and inquired about being a military policeman. The recruiter said I could join the army with a guaranteed MOS code (military occupational specialty) for the military police corps. The requirements included a background check, successfully completing basic military training, then graduating from a military police academy in Fort Gordon, Georgia.

On my eighteenth birthday, I traveled to Roanoke, Virginia and joined the Army. About fifty young men stood in ranks at attention, giving an oath to faithfully serve our country. Instantly the shouting of orders began. Within minutes, we were boarding a Trailways bus, nonstop to Fort Jackson, South Carolina.

My military experience was certainly challenging, yet educational and rewarding. Discipline and commands were similar at home so I adapted more easily than most. Within a couple of weeks the wimps were weeded out and sent home. The biggest adjustments for me were the hotter temperatures, pine needles, snakes, and mess hall food. Yuk!

I arrived back in Amherst proudly wearing my uniform. The Burley Hollow boy was the talk of the town. My head shaved and shiny white teeth with no cavities, I looked sharp — and felt proud too. I was home on furlough for a week, just finishing up basic training;

then I'd be heading out for military police training in Georgia.

Nothing was ever discussed at home regarding the military. It was folklore that my dad was drafted, serving part of his tour in France. I never saw Army photos or discharge papers related to him. He never talked of his role in the military and I never asked. I knew that my uncle Jack served in the Army and was killed fighting in World War I. My uncle's tombstone is the tallest in our family cemetery plot.

My first days attending the eight-week military police academy confirmed that this was a career path that I wanted. I realized that I enjoyed serving and dealing with people. Only two weeks remained before we were to graduate and this high school dropout is one of the top-ranked privates in the class. Learning, for the first time, was enjoyable and stimulating.

With one week remaining, the School Commander called us to formation on the assembly field. His announcement pertained to our assignment orders. Anticipation overwhelmed every one of us as we stood at attention. Then the unexpected — "The last class received orders for stateside military bases. Everyone in this class is going to Germany or South Korea." Shit! — My heart froze. The Captain paused, then said, "There are only two orders that will keep your young ass in the United States — one is to sign up for CID (Criminal Investigative Division) school and second, Airborne Jump School."

Damn, I'd never been near an airplane. Jump School? What the hell was jump school? I knew Germany and South Korea are very far away! — I would never see Edith again. We had two days to decide, stateside or abroad.

Again, I returned home in my crisp uniform, this time proudly wearing my military police crossed pistols on each collar. And yes, I had received orders for jump school. In a few days I would leave for Fort Benning, South Carolina, where the real kick-ass training began.

Three intensive weeks of jump school confirmed that my self-confidence was far greater than it appeared to be years earlier. Everything had changed for me. I was telling the folks back home that the Army was the best thing to happen to me. There is one moment that every jump school soldier never forgets — that first jump out of an airplane flying at 150 knots and an altitude of 1300 feet. My first jump was also my first flight. Flying in a C-130, we approached the drop zone. The Jump Master yelled, "Stand up! Hook up! Prepare to jump! — GO!" If anyone had the slightest hesitation as he entered the door, the Jump Master would stick his boot in his ass and kick him out!

The day I joined the Army, I had no knowledge of the legendary unit known as the 101st Airborne Division. Wanting to be a police officer had zero similarity to jumping from flying airplanes. My five required jumps were successful and jump school was history. My choice for assignment was the 101st. The Airborne School Commander side stepped to each paratrooper, pinning our wings on our uniform. As fresh young paratroopers, we felt bold with guts of elitism. My orders arrived immediately after the ceremony. Effective 0600 hours tomorrow I would be a "Screaming Eagle" with the 101st Airborne Division.

The ceremonial-issued wings became my "blood wings." To attest and confirm the honor to wear airborne wings, a ritual ruled the night. I took my Army issued wings and removed the clamps, inserting the pins into my chest, causing myself to bleed. As blood ran down my chest, I dabbed the wings in my blood, allowing it to dry. Decades later, as the funeral service was beginning, and my Dad's casket was being closed, I walked up and leaned over, slipping my blood wings under his hands. A token of my pride as my tears dripped on his suit.

Prior to arriving at my new assignment, orders were clear and concise that my unit insignia patches must be sewn on every uniform. I entered the main gates at Fort Campbell, Kentucky proudly wearing my dress uniform with polished cross pistols and the acclaimed screaming eagle patch.

Intense military training had altered my domestic profile as a new groom. I realized all the attention and focus on learning had put some real emotional distance between me and my new bride. During these military months, Edith had been living with her parents, occasionally staying out at the Burley farm. She felt very little love for the mountains, but discovered my mom's kindness and enjoyed her Southern home-cooked meals.

It was amazing that in such a short time much had been accomplished. From being a blundering teenager who quit school and got married, to joining the military, and jumping from planes, I was now an Airborne Military Policeman in excellent physical shape with a huge nose and pretty teeth.

A sense of stability was evident. Still a private, I was prohibited to live off post. I was living in the barracks assigned to a squad, performing post patrol and working the main gate. I had to be the sharpest of the sharp to get the main gate detail. Eye contact, a firm voice, and a precise salute were essential. Generals and battalion commanders were generally nice. It was the young lieutenants and some cocky captains that acted like dip shits.

A defining moment occurred shortly after I arrived at Fort Campbell. My company commander, Captain R. C. Mehciz, unexpectantly requested me to report to his office. Captains rarely command privates report to their office. Was this about Edith? Had there been a death in my family? I stood before him, frozen at attention. He ordered me at ease and pointed to a chair.

Captain Mehciz proceeded to say how impressed he was with me, praising my performance. He continued by saying he saw my potential for leadership, suggesting I give strong consideration to making my career in the Army, and possibly attaining command assignments.

The Captain proceeded to inform me that he had discovered in my records that I didn't have a high school diploma. His compliments to me were inspiring and challenging. I accepted his advice and began attending night classes at a high school on base. Several months later at a school ceremony, I proudly accepted my military GED diploma from Captain Mehciz.

The following month, orders were cut for my first promotion to private first class. A year later, I completed a traffic investigation course from Northwestern Institute and was promoted to Specialist 4th Class. My new assignment was traffic accident investigations off post, including fatalities involving military personnel.

Highway 41, a fifty-mile stretch from Fort Campbell to Nashville, had the highest automobile accident fatality statistics in the state of Tennessee. Speed, alcohol, and death were triplets that stole the lives of many paratroopers.

Months before my tour ended, I was promoted to Sergeant and became a squad leader. Captain Mehciz observed qualities in me far greater than I realized I had.

My company commander, was a West Point graduate (I think), a paratrooper, and ranger – who led an elite unit of military police officers. He gave me something I rarely or never received in Burley Hollow. Capt. Mehciz's praise and encouragement validated my individuality. To this very day, when being recognized or receiving honors, I become emotional. It's truly overwhelming, yet it is also understandable. As a child, I yearned for acknowledgment, yet only received silence and experienced heartfelt hurt.

Joining the military and its rewarding experience changed my life. My parents never said to me, "We are proud of you!" — I think they were. My thanks to both of them and Company Commander, Captain Mehciz. — Airborne! Yesterday is forgiven —

My Father

Two black limousines traveled slowly out of Burley Hollow, kicking up a light trail of dust. Unbearable September heat and the high noon sun reflected off the chrome and crystal black metal. Sardis Methodist Church was already overflowing. The church organist was playing hymns of The Old Rugged Cross and Rock of Ages. My Dad was a member and attended this church his entire life. Today was his last visit. His body lay peacefully near the altar in the best suit he had ever worn. Flowers in abundance, from near and far, surrounded his casket.

Our immediate family sat in silence as the limousines slowly roll along the mountain highway toward the church. We came upon three families of colored folks walking along the side of the highway, dressed in their Sunday best. The elders had their suit coats slung over their shoulders, their shirts saturated with sweat. It was Ed Morris and his family, and extended members of two black families that had walked for more than a mile to pay their respects to my father. Upon our arrival at the church, I ordered the two funeral home drivers to immediately return and pick all of them up. Those families, despite the heat and distance walked, demonstrated their admiration for my father. This was humbling to me.

We witnessed an outpouring of love and heartfelt condolences that day. It was a day of deep sadness, a testament of genuine honor and respect for Ernest Bentley Burley, a poor and simple man — my father.

For me to live a quality life of tomorrow I had to heal from the pains of yesterday. Much work awaited me to acquire a renewed quality of well being. The focus and objectives were well established from my psychological sessions at the Medical College of Virginia. There was a uniqueness about me that many, unfortunately, never grasped. Tremendous effort and focus must be applied by the patient to seek a better quality of life. I had to work at it, and pray for it. I had to taste the sweetness of inner peace and feel my mental burdens become weightless. I had to feel the hurt and despair of yesterday. Eventually, as I fought to free myself, my soul softened to calm and the scars began to heal within my heart.

Children are influenced by one or both of their parents. In many regards I credit my characteristics to both. I didn't truly know my father until long after he died. Reluctantly, after my insistent questioning, my mom revealed many of her childhood experiences that helped me better understand her way of thinking. To find out who they were, I had to open their windows and search their rooms of experience. How were they raised? What scars did they take to their grave? How on earth could they give praise when they never received it. They could not say, "I love you," when those exact words were never expressed to them. The revelations were far beyond one's imagination. My dysfunctional traits continued to negatively influence my parenting during the first marriage. I confess that I experienced many parental short comings while raising my young children.

The nurture that I denied Douglas, Dorrie, and Donald was the same that was denied to me. Unfortunately, that dysfunctional cycle continued.

I remained at home for eighteen years. I cannot remember my parents ever being away from home at night. Our family ate breakfast in the kitchen. Dinner and supper were served in the dining room. Dad gave the blessing. We always ate in silence. During the summer, with longer daylight, supper was between eight and nine. During the winter months supper was around six. After dessert Mom cleared off the table, and Dad headed to bed. Nights — were long and silent.

Growing up around relatives, who exercised little to no conversation among themselves and even less with children, were a major dysfunctional trait. Yet, we as children accepted it as a norm, knowing no difference.

As I approached my late 20's, the demons of childhood began to rear their heads. Clashing full force was a self-realization of the emptiness, hurt, guilt, and emotional slush in the pit of my stomach. This began to impact my professional career. At that time I didn't have the slightest suspicion that any of this was connected to my dad. There also were additional demons pointing directly to my own mistakes.

Dad blessed me with untold gifts of knowledge. I never went hungry, always had clothes to wear and always felt safe. He taught by silence, never explaining anything. He placed upon me the expectation to do things as he did. I learned to split fire wood by watching him. Trust me, there is an art in splitting wood. I learned the proper way to pick or twist fruits from its stem. Some I pulled, some I twisted. Watching him, I mastered rolling my fingers around the cow's teats for maximum milk flow. At 12, I knew exactly where the bullet was supposed to enter the hog's head — between the eyes and one inch up with a slight downward projection.

To this day, I benefit to the fullest for all the rewarding knowledge I learned from him. It provided me with a strong sense of independence. I have saved untold dollars by performing construction, carpentry, and home repairsmyself.

The most valued gift I gave Nicholas, my son from my second marriage, was my time. Our time — togetherness. That father-son bonding. That very same gift didn't exist with my children of the first marriage. This foundation of bonding is essential for child development and parental nourishment. During quiet times, reflecting on my childhood, the thing most missed, and most needed and even prayed for, is time, our time. — Time with my father.

His life was his farm. His life was cattle, tobacco, growing pretty red tomatoes and juicy peaches! That's all he knew. My transition to accepting him as he was and forgiving him for his weaknesses was from researching his childhood and adult life. It's inconceivable that beginning at the age of 10, I was always alone, building dams in small creeks, fishing and hunting wild game. My father never indicated an interest in hunting. The only time we were together in the mountains was repairing property line fences caused by tree damage. I toted the water bucket and ham biscuits. Of the thousand-plus squirrels I killed, we never skinned one together.

At 10, baseball was my passion. I played two seasons with the Connie Mack Little League out of

Lynchburg. Some games were missed because working on the farm took precedence over sports. My father never pitched baseball with me. Never! My pitching buddy was four cement steps leading up to our front porch. Baseballs were restricted, but tennis or rubber balls were permissible. I didn't dare kill the grass pitching from the same spot. My target was the third step. When the ball hit the step, it would bounce back as a grounder and I would scoop it up and repeat the throw. I played the position of shortstop well.

On Saturdays, when our Little League team played at the old Amherst school, Dad usually sold produce nearby on Main Street from the tailgate of his pickup. Playing shortstop, I kept my eyes on the batter, while frequently glancing across the field. I have many memories of anticipating that he would pull up in his old truck to watch me play. I wanted so much for him to see me dive and catch a hot grounder and fire it to first base for an out. He never came.

The game was over, yet the hot sun lingered above. Carrying my glove and cleats, I walked to where Dad sold his fruit and vegetables. He had gone. I continued walking several blocks to the traffic circle. It was a fun day and I got to play baseball. An ice-cold Coca Cola and peanuts would have been nice but I had no money. The thought, however, was refreshing. Water from the gas station water hose would suffice.

From the town circle to my front yard, there are seven miles of highway and more than a mile of dirt road sprinkled with gravel. I hoped my right thumb would get lucky and quickly hitchhike me a ride. This boy was hungry. Hopefully, the motorist would know me and take me all the way home. I realized there was a good chance I may be dropped off at the highway, and I walk home — in silence.

* * * * *

A huge Weeping Willow tree stood near our front porch. The enjoyable memories associated with this tree are many. Each spring, Baltimore Orioles arrived and built their unique nests on the long dangling branches. The thick green foliage camouflaged the radiant orange and black feathers of the parents as they fed and protected their baby chicks. These beautiful birds were a community attraction.

Dad liked his colorful birds. On Sunday afternoon, folks would drive up to see them. He would proudly claim ownership while pointing to their well-concealed nests. They built their hanging nest only in this type of tree. We had the only willow in the hollow! Throughout summer this tree blessed us with plentiful shade. On many Sundays, after church, the children would get an old quilt and spread it across the grass and play. The cool mountain breeze would gently sway the branches across our faces and tickle our necks.

Unfortunately, this tree's majestic images also were greatly tarnished with painful childhood memories. A weeping willow branch, with all of its leaves stripped, was known to me as a "switch." It was an effective object to inflict pain, and even cause skin welts, when it lashed upon a child's legs.

His words were few, "Go get me a switch." Hell, my dad might be down at the corn house or out back at the woodshed. We could be finishing up supper! He set

40

the tone, he set the time, and proceeded to whip me with little or no discussion. I don't recall every whipping and I don't remember there being many. However, when I did receive one, it was logged in my memory bank for quite some time. There were two lashings I'll never forget.

As I returned to him with a branch in hand, I dared to inquire what I had done to deserve this excruciating punishment. I remember his heightened anger once as I handed him a branch. I was around eight and he was 54! In his scornful tone, cursing, while stripping away the leaves, he ordered me to get him a bigger branch. I thought, "This is not good." The larger the branch was, the higher the chance for painful welts. I was an expert in selecting a delicate branch, creating less of a sting on my legs. My dad became wise to my choice, having the knowledge that the more durable the switch, the more painful the lash. He seemed to always pick a time when I was wearing shorts! "Time out" or going to bed without dessert would have been an excellent alternative.

Walking toward my dad, taking him a willow branch knowing he was about to strip it down and turn it into a weapon to cause pain, was most unsettling. It was truly terrorizing! He would grab my wrist with one hand, preventing escape and begin to lash my tender legs, causing me to run in circles, screaming from the switch's sting. "Stand still, dammit!" Mom was nowhere in sight – she never was.

This emotional and physical pain is only a memory now. My home and the willow tree are gone. Remembering the burning stings, swelling welts and my wrist locked in his grip as I circled him, while high stepping in agony, was all part of a Burley Hollow culture of punishment. I had an older cousin who said she was "gettin' a whippin" because she refused to stop dating a boy who had poor teeth and chewed tobacco.

My father left much deeper stings and scars on my heart. There is no question that his whippings were emotionally hurtful, but they impacted my self esteem far more. His style of punishment created a sense of subconscious fear. As years passed my demons of yesterday became restless.

As I reflect on the decades past, I see my father's actions as his method of discipline based on his inability to establish a dialogue. Our home place was the only one in the hollow that had an old-fashioned damson grove with about fifteen trees. One day he discovered that while I was picking damsons, I had broken off a small limb atop the fruit tree. He became furious and unleashed a tirade of profanity. I was a child, maybe 13, standing on a homemade ladder twelve feet in the air, reaching beyond my limits. The ladder slipped and broke the limb. This was a typical incident of his scorn. He walked away in silence, leaving me likewise. Moments like these devastated me!

One Saturday, my cousin Phyllis and I collectively picked eleven bushels of damsons. We neatly lined the full baskets in a row to proudly display our harvest. Dad came home and saw our remarkable harvest. There was no smile – no expression of amazement. Our anticipated praises from him were whispers in the wind — we never heard them!

As I became older, I looked forward to riding with Dad on Saturday mornings as he hauled his produce to town. He proudly displayed his harvest — tomatoes, corn, string beans, damsons, peaches, squash, cucumbers, and potatoes, I enjoyed the adults smiling and talking to me as I assisted Dad with making the sales. It was cool to sell a thirty-five-cent basket of peaches and receive a silver dollar!

This particular Saturday, I was up early and had eaten breakfast with my mom and dad. I anticipated leaving with him, heading out with his pickup already loaded the night before. We were walking to the truck and out of nowhere he said,

"Stay here and cut the grass." Well, this was a kick to my stomach.

"Cut the grass" is a really big deal for someone about 13. My home had two acres of yard, and I was using a push mower. I pushed while the wheels rolled along over the yard and caused the fifteen inch blades to rotate, cutting the blades of grass. This was an overwhelming task demanding lots of exertion for a boy my size.

Mom kept an eye on me. She would come out with a dampened rag and some sweet ice tea. It took most of the day to conquer this chore. I lay down under the willow tree, exhausted, with the mower nearby. High humidity and temperatures quickly whipped up lightning, thunder and frontal winds. Mom hollered from the front porch to get inside.

Shortly thereafter the weather cleared and the sun came back out. The yard looked pristine with its neatly cut grass and a refreshing shower of rain. I didn't see my dad arrive home but I heard him from a distance. As he walked from the pickup shed toward the house he spotted the mower under the willow tree. I had failed to place it back inside the barn, keeping it protected from the weather.

This time his profanity and abusiveness will always be remembered as his ultimate of rage and belittlement. Every step I took that day was all I could muster pushing the mower. Not one blade of grass was skipped over a two-acre area, — and he cussed me out for leaving the mower under the tree.

Many years later, in 1971, during a chilly February night, our home was gutted by a fire, leaving only its rock chimney towering to the heavens. The cement steps, once leading to the front porch, now led to a heap of ashes. The weeping willow perished from the intense heat. Months earlier the lovely orioles had departed for South America.

This man, my dear father, had given me so much that many dream of having. Yet sadly, this highly respected gentleman of kindness, faith, and integrity walked this earth with anger manifested from the secrets of his childhood. I truly feel my dad's heart was not malicious. I wonder so often what he endured during his younger days. How much sunlight and warmth of kindness entered his room of experience? Dad hurt me deeply in so many ways and yet, my admiration, honor and respect for him are unwavering. I'm thankful that despite the silence, he was home every day and every night. Whether my dad was nearby on the farm, or asleep in his bed, he gave me surety. Many children today are not blessed to have that.

I remember the day when we had our first father-son talk, not far from Burley Hollow. The sun was setting behind the trees than lined the Sardis cemetery. He had been dead for 15 years. I sat upon his grave near his foot stone. I was in my 40's but felt more like I was fifteen. I sat in silence for a long time. I was nervous and felt intimidated as I struggled for words, trembling with emotions. I felt my father's presence was ever so real. Our first talk was beautiful and fulfilling, and our first moments together blessed me with a sliver of God's reward.

The sun seemed still, lingering in place, giving me a little more light and rays of warmth. In time darkness came as I stood up, and the breeze yielded to a quietness. I would return soon when we could talk some more. I thanked him for listening — I felt his appreciation for my visit. I turned to leave, tears dripping on his grave.

I thought I saw a Baltimore Oriole —

EULOGY

Its quiet now-. Just moments away from the break of light, yet the crickets, and the distant cow bell gently sounds across the dew covered grass. Surrounded by life, and its wonders and also its sorrows. My thoughts as I sit here, feeling the coolness of the silent dropping dew, are without limitations.

Sure it hurts, and yet I can smile, and have no feelings of illness. I can think as clear as the sky now shows its stars. I know I'll cry again today and the pain, again, will visit my heart, but that in time, will go away.

He was a man that words, in total, I cannot express. He had, to his death, the traditional honesty, kindness and gentlemanship that many today cannot be identified with.

Ernest Bentley Burley was a good christian man, a hard working and providing father, Yes,-he is my father, and I am forever, proud to be his son.

Pre-dawn September 18, 1971

Cornerstone of Healing

When Captain Bennett transported me to the 7th floor psychiatric unit at the Medical College of Virginia Hospital, I knew exactly where he was taking me. Our police patrol officers frequently served mental warrants. These warrants were judicially issued documents authorizing the apprehension and confinement of an individual in a medical facility until an assessment hearing could be held. Almost always, two officers served the commonly known "green warrant" on an individual then handcuffed the person for safety and prevention of injury. Bennett was taking me to the very same unit that I, on many occasions, had delivered mental individuals in need of counseling.

Many years earlier, MCV became an integral part of my medical battles when fighting ulcerative colitis. This intestinal bleeding with bouts of abdominal pain started in 1970. For a decade, Dr. Alvin M. Zfass and his team fought this disabling disease. They continuously did research and tried new efforts to slow the degree of inflammation and bleeding. Monthly follow up exams at the hospital and rotating work shifts created stressful times. Within a couple of years, as my condition worsened, a steroid called Prednisone became my primary drug to battle this illness. At periodic times I took 90 mg per day, and at the same time was working a patrol beat assignment. This was not wise! Everyone was committed to beating this condition. A high dosage of Prednisone slowed the bleeding. As we lowered the dose, the blood flow would rise. We named this treatment "seesaw hell." Sulfasalazine was prescribed for slowing down the inflammation and protecting the intestinal lining. When bleeding became excessive, 40 cc's of Cortisone rectal insertions and a new drug called Imuran became the big guns for treatment. One battle became three — one being Colitis, the second being the side effects of Prednisone, and the third was a courageous effort to continue patrolling my beat.

* * * * *

There was a consensus by many who witnessed my tailspin and saw my foundation of existence clearly crumble. Friends best described me as "damaged goods – a broken man – an image of heartbroken despair." All are reasonable descriptive terms. The scars and silence of childhood, the abuse, failures, medical battles, and domestic dysfunction, incorporated with a forced disability retirement were the missiles that took me out. My thoughts and plans to commit suicide — to take my life — seemed the only option. To me, it seemed I had no life to take.

As I now reflect pass to those times thirty-five years ago, I see a beautiful transition from that time in my life to today. I see a structure of renewed life, a purpose, confidence, a life of peace, pride, and achievement. I'm thankful that I became a better person from my ruins of a half century ago.

Cornerstones are found throughout the world. Scripture writings describe Jesus Christ as the cornerstone of faith. Structures built thousands of years ago in ancient Egypt and Greece are still towering today because of a well-laid cornerstone foundation. History attests they are essential in freemasonry. I now have a cornerstone!

Mine, however, is different. It's not a chiseled stone or poured concrete slab for me to stand upon. It is a wall-to-wall cornerstone providing support to my pillars toward rebuilding my life. The key corners of my stone of healing are faith and mankind.

James L. Levenson ,M.D.

If you have lived in the Richmond metropolitan area for some time, then you are familiar with a commonly known phrase, "If there is something really wrong with you, MCV is the place to go." I believe this 100%! I don't know if it was luck of the draw or my unique mental circumstances, but Dr. Levenson became the lead psychiatrist in my therapy recovery team. At that time, he was the Assistant Professor of Psychiatry & Medicine. I rate him as the gold standard in the specialized profession of Psychiatry. Jim Levenson became a part of my cornerstone from the first session with him.

My foundation was solidified by Dr. Levenson as weeks and months passed with daily counseling sessions during hospitalization, then weekly sessions upon discharge. A key factor in our joint effort to seek a new quality of life was establishing mutual trust. His low profile and calm demeanor were traits of his effectiveness. Dr. Levenson is a quiet gentleman who still today, squirrels throughout the large medical campus, drawing little or no attention to himself. The most valuable trait I picked up from him was his way of listening during our sessions. Jim Levenson was a master in getting you to let your painful emotions flow from your soul. I applied his style of listening as I traveled back to my childhood community in Amherst, Virginia.

For the first eighteen months I was on his leash. As my stability improved, he allowed me to run free. We trusted each other's assessments and judgments. He knew that I was devoting many hours to confronting the demons of my past. He also believed I had established goals toward getting well. As the months passed, the frequency for sessions became less. Dr. Levenson would target a certain scar or dysfunctional issue and we would devote total attention to that specific issue until it was sufficiently resolved. His approach to progressive counseling at a respectful pace and the art of listening is his legacy. He is the epitome of excellence in his field of psychiatry.

I know he is always there. My need for him is only a phone call away. I'm proud to acknowledge that I haven't needed a session with Dr. Levenson in decades. His cornerstone of professional contributions helped me build new confidence, with my pride and sunshine aglow! My many accomplishments and current way of living a renewed quality of life can be directly credited to Dr. James Lloyd Levenson, his department of Psychiatry, and the Medical College of Virginia Hospital.

Rebecca & Steve Ogden

Family members in Amherst were mostly unaware of my many medical and mental issues. We were 100 miles apart and living two distinctly different lifestyles. My mother and my three teenage children visited me while I was still hospitalized. While in intensive care, a hospital official request was made that my brother-in-law travel to Richmond and take possession of all firearms in my home. Strict instructions were given to keep them secure and under his control until at some time later it might be deemed safe to return them to me. This instruction was without an objection. The totality of this revelation seemed complex to my family and difficult for them to comprehend. Everyone seemed silent in what to say or how to help.

The following weeks immediately after leaving the hospital were crucial times. Nutritional food, rest, and family support were keys to rebuilding. My sister Rebecca and her husband Steve built a home on a small tract of land that once was a part of our farm, so it felt good to be back in Burley Hollow. They opened their home to me and provided food in abundance, much of which my sister learned to prepare from our mom. Steve also held his own culinary talents.

Steve had a huge custom-designed wood stove in his basement. It was made from 1/4 inch steel and was about 30 inches long. He kept a large pot of water on top of the stove to give off moisture. Heat from a wood stove and steam rising from that water gave me the ultimate experience of comfort. Each of their rooms above had 12-inch vent grills in the floor. Warm heat rises, so by design it was perfect and allowed natural flow heating throughout the home. They placed a twin-size bed in the basement for me. With a cozy wood fire and prime country cookin' this boy was tickled. This setup gave me total privacy and quietness, and allowed me to focus on my objectives at hand.

Some days, I wrote letters to people for hours. My first step toward healing in the basement was writing a very long letter to my first wife, Edith Mae. Not long after I typed the final draft, I went to Lynchburg to visit her and deliver my letter. Our children eventually received copies.

Edith and I talked for two hours. We cried, laughed, and accepted our failures of the past. We criticized with resolve, shared disappointments, and forgave each other for our misgivings during our marriage. The acceptance of our past and our forgiveness to each other was commendable. My departing hug was long, as we embraced in silence. Sobbing, Edith whispered, "We could have done better."

Rebecca and Steve's love, and hospitalities were components of my cornerstone. The weeks living with them gave me a step-off point to brighter days. They provided me a sense of security and warmth from their firewood, and their comforting foods. Seeing the mountains behind their home where I hunted squirrels, all were cornerstones of healing.

Captain Thomas A. Clark

A difficult and fearful challenge that lies ahead was the disconnect — a feeling of abandonment from my law enforcement family. Things that had been the tools of my profession were no longer in my life. The norms of my career and little things I took for granted just vanished. There was the enjoyable interaction with people, stopping by to check on a grocery store owner. Daily roll call, inspections, my patrol unit, the gun belt, and the unexpected when on duty are now just memories. These components of my police career were now gone! I knew this would be painful because working the streets of Richmond was my life. Residents from Fulton Bottom to Church Hill, from down on the Pike up to Willow Oaks were a part of me.

At the time of my retirement, I didn't personally know Captain Clark. We had met once at some police officer's funeral, and I recall we had once exchanged greetings during National Police Week ceremonies. He was a veteran police officer assigned to a command position serving with the adjoining Henrico County Police. The working relationship between our two police agencies was respectful and considered excellent.

There was an oversight in my thinking that I only had to focus on yesterday and rebuild from the past. I didn't consider the overwhelming impact the severance from my fellow officers would have upon me. In my experience, police officers are noted to be compassionate professionals. But when we screw up, condemnation and gossip rule the day. When we hurt or struggle, brotherhood is prevalent.

While it was confirmed, that I was doing well in self-recovery and keeping Dr. Levenson abreast of my progress, the absence of belonging as disheartening. I truly felt lost. Clark had been active for years, playing a major role with the Virginia State Crime Clinic. Its membership consisted of law enforcement officers of agencies throughout the Commonwealth of Virginia. Agencies such as the F.B.I., Secret Service, State Police, Sheriff and Police Departments, including private security members, made up the organization. Tom Clark's leadership and respect by his peers earned him the honor to serve as the 24th President, (1986) - of the Central Virginia Chapter, of our State Crime Clinic.

Learning of my situation, President Clark extended an invitation to me to attend a future monthly meeting. His delicate approach and invitation placed no pressure upon me to be his guest. I attended a meeting shortly thereafter. I felt odd, sort of out of place and incomplete, as we mingled before the luncheon. I didn't expect the respect and warmth as handshakes with "welcome back" softened the anxiety. Almost everyone knew I recently had been released from a hospital psychiatric unit. I previously had been a member in good standing, but my dues had expired and my membership was suspended.

As the months passed, my attendance at the meetings continued. I quickly realized being in the presence of my peers was good supportive therapy. Upon arrival at our meetings, I would walk up and thank Clark. His simple invitation meant more to me than he ever realized. That first year, the members elected me to be Sergeant at Arms. Having that position made me a board member with specific duties.

Our Central Virginia Chapter was strong. The leaders of the preceding 23 years had established a vibrant networking between the many agencies in and surrounding the capital of Virginia. Meetings were always productive with attendees exchanging sensitive and vital information in person. A side benefit of our meetings was a creation of professional bonding. With future contacts, I now had a face in memory when that fellow member or officer answered the phone.

During the following years, things happened far beyond any vision of my expectations. The membership elected me 2nd vice-president, then 1st vice-president the following year. In 1989, they exercised their confidence and trust and voted me the 27th president of our Chapter.

Captain Tom Clark's support, his confidence, and encouragement blessed me with things I had lost long ago. His leadership, supported with membership respect gave me hope. Clark's cornerstone was a rebuilding of my self-worth. He helped me realize my renewed potential. His reaching out now made me part of something that gave me a purpose and inspiration. I had been a patrolman my entire career. Once a broken man with no badge, and no tour of duty, I now stood steely at the podium presiding over a Crime Clinic meeting. There they sat, educated professionals with years of experience, chiefs, sheriffs, captains, federal agents, and others. I was their leader with gavel in hand. President Burley called the meeting to order, standing proud and confident, and standing on Tom Clark's cornerstone!

Captain Thomas W. Shook

Early one morning, my telephone rang. I answered not fully awake. It was Tom Shook, and he was calling with an invitation to join him for lunch. I took this as rather unexpected, but I honored his request, and we met a few days later. He was a fellow officer serving with me on the Richmond Bureau of Police. We didn't have a close connection during our years of working together. Shook had brothers that were Richmond officers, one retired as a detective. We were assigned different shifts and different divisions. I worked patrol, and his career had mostly been traffic enforcement and safety. Like

Clark, Shook had moved up through the ranks to Captain. He had a profile more descriptive as a pastor than a patrol officer. Reticent, displaying poise in his actions Captain Shook was known among his peers as a man of faith, and unquestionable character.

He allowed me to lead the dialogue during lunch, with an occasional question. Like Dr. Levenson, he put me at ease as he calmly listened. Our lunch and discussions held that day were significant game-changers for me then, and even today.

Shook posed a question never addressed during my hospitalization. His question: "Using a day as a measurement, where do you think you are in life."

Feeling pessimistic, pausing in silence I replied, "Daylight has yielded and darkness is near."

Shook, shaking his head slowly in disagreement, "No — no, your life has just been renewed, and you're only in your early forties. You have a toddler son, Nicholas." I stared at him in helpless silence. "Glen, you're at high noon."

Before we departed, we shared a prayer for healing, asking God for perseverance, faith, and patience. He thanked him for giving me the strength and courage to prevail. He reassured me he was there if I needed him. I thanked him.

Captain Shook's five words "Glen, you're at high noon" was a revelation of a perspective I had never given a moment of consideration. His words and vision were pertinent to the realization of my future contributions to my son, and to society.

I'm proud to claim the productive path I have traveled since Shook and I shared lunch more than 30 years ago! These two police captains unknowingly reinforced my professional counseling at MCV by sharing simple wisdom and practical application toward helping a fellow officer and friend stand tall again.

Recently I took the opportunity during our monthly meeting and asked to be recognized by our Richmond Police Retirees president. I paced between some thirty-five retirees and spoke for 10 minutes about this "officer" meeting me years ago. Becoming a little emotional, I told my story like it is written here.

I praised him in the presence of his fellow retirees. I pointed to Tom Shook and called out his name as he sat a few feet away.

It has been a while since "high noon," but daylight continues to bless my life every day. I don't seek the darkness, but it will come in due time.

Jesus Christ

No matter the mountain's height, nor the ocean's depth, the power of faith is the foremost component of my success and well-being. To have reached that pinnacle and stood upon a cornerstone of Jesus Christ — is a milestone moment of my time.

Since that darkest day of my career, the last day as a police officer, my mountain of challenges has been conquered. For some 12,434 days Jesus Christ has been the Chairman of my Board. His gavel to gavel love and his nearness have helped keep me in a sunny room of experience.

I stand anointed with blessings aplenty. The foundation of these blessings and the healing of my past sit upon the cornerstone of my faith in Jesus Christ, upon Jim Levenson, Tom Clark, Tom Shook, Rebecca and Steve, and countless others who prayed for and believed in me.

DOMINOES

Rising before me was an unprecedented task. This was an indescribable challenge to be undertaken and with no road map provided for achievement. I was now free from confinement and intense counseling in the psychiatric unit. No more workshop sessions that dissected my emotions, revealing my deepest scars of darkness.

The most emotional moment during my hospital commitment was the day before I was discharged. Entering my room alone, neatly dressed and wearing a long white hospital jacket, this seasoned psychiatrist pulled up a chair near my bed. "I came by for a few minutes to meet you." Giving no introduction, his heartfelt smile while reaching to shake my hand gave me comfort. This day was different. My counseling team of six never made their daily rounds that particular morning. These specialists were assigned to me immediately upon hospitalization. They were aware tomorrow was my discharge date, and it was going to be the best day of my new life.

"You were a Richmond Police officer, right?" the doctor asked.

"Yes, 23 years." I replied.

He was unknowingly playing me, getting a feel for my stability, and evaluating my response.

"Were you a captain, chief?"

"No," I replied, with a slight humble smile, "Just a patrolman."

He continued, "What did people call you?"

"Most called me Officer Burley, others greeted me as Patrolman," I explained.

He leaned near. His face, a portrait of sincerity. "So — who are you today?"

I began to tremble as the seconds ticked away. My next seven words were the most difficult I remember ever having to say. A seizure-like experience overcame me with overwhelming emotion. A moment in time had frozen. I felt helpless getting my answer past my lips. I struggled to seek composure as my eyes glazed over with tears.

"I guess — I am just Glen Burley."

The doctor walked away and returned with some tissues. He reached out with his right hand and took mine. Our hands were clasped as he waited for me to wipe my face. This moment was unchartered waters. I remember his eyes held compassion but firmness. His smile returned as he reaffirmed his handshake.

"Mister Glen Burley, it's my honor to meet you."

* * * * *

Dominos have been around for centuries. The Chinese are thought to be the first to play this game, using small rectangular objects derived from bones and elephant tusks around 1100 A.D. Eight hundred years later, I don't think any made their way into my neighborhood. If they did, someone snatched them up.

My first memory of seeing modern-day dominos was in an old hotel near a railroad station in Monroe, Virginia. During their transfer and layovers, it was a game of past time among the many railway employees staying in this hotel.

Monroe was a village centerpiece for one attraction – lots of trains. The train station also was a repair and transfer facility. In the summer, my Dad would park his pickup near the tracks and the train passengers would step off and purchase fresh peaches or garden produce. I would scamper up to the hotel, venture inside, and be amazed at this high-ceilinged room where long tables were occupied with grubby looking railroad men playing dominos. To this day, I cannot describe the specifics of how the game is played. For an unexplainable reason, I selected dominos as a recovery tool to establish a renewed quality of life.

As expected, the longer I was a patient in the psychiatric unit, the more I realized how much better I felt. The unit provided excellent food nutrition, with structured hours of therapy and an opportunity for sufficient sleep. For weeks during our team round table discussions, I would write notes with the most significant and impacting points that scarred my soul. Tucked away in my coat pocket were little sheets of paper that listed these major issues, awaiting my confrontation.

The time had come to ride my demons, one at a time. I knew full well I needed to grab my ass with both hands, ride hard, and go to work. Oh no, this self-healing process wasn't something that I slept on overnight, then awoke the next morning feeling all bright-eyed and bushy-tailed. I also knew full well that this ride would be emotional, exhausting, and demanding. My timeline of this ride would be determined by my efficiency in revealing the sunshine from the darkness of yesterday.

There in a silent pause, I stood staring at sixteen shiny, black dominos! No bones, or ivory – just simply wood. These little objects, towering like mini Stonehenge monuments, were neatly lined up across my bookshelf. They would become my rehabilitative aids for months, extending into years. I wanted tomorrow's journey to be visual. I believed that seeing evidence of my progress would stimulate my enthusiasm to push onward.

During my last week of hospitalization, I had already begun to tackle an issue that needed immediate attention. It involved another veteran police officer who was much more than just that — we were the best of friends. In years past, we both had been presidents of Richmond's Fraternal Order of Police. We had collectively made many strides toward improving Richmond police officers' quality of employment. A couple of years earlier our relationship shattered when we differed in our viewpoints of how to best convey our plight to city government.

He pissed me off, and I stopped speaking to him. Not good! I refused to acknowledge him when we crossed paths at headquarters, or in social functions. My stubborn attitude and the inability to dissolve this friction were unbearable and awkward for both of us.

The green team had applied every professional approach to get me ready for discharge. They were confident and I was too. The hospital extended a professional courtesy to me and, per my request, they made contact with this officer to come and visit me.

Within an hour, there he stood in my hospital room doorway. It was time to make amends. It appeared surprising to him to witness my frail profile. We assured the floor nurse that we would be fine in a private setting and she closed the door. This officer saw a different man. I was smiling a little. He sat and we chatted, then he listened to my summary presentation of contriteness. My apologies to him were accepted and his forgiveness of me validated the beauty of understanding and the value of our friendship.

He has lived in Oregon for decades. Now thousands of miles separate us, but our bond has become even stronger. Years later, we stay in touch and see each other at our annual police retirees' reunion. Through time, we both have become seasoned men and value our honor. Our respect for each other is priceless.

This was my first amazing and mentally uplifting experience to embrace the peace that grew from his hospital visit. Our accomplishment ruled the day! Sgt. Robert E. Walker was my first domino! It was such a rewarding experience to lay that first domino down. As each one became horizontal, it verified another confirmation of healing. Finding that peace within thyself can be invigorating,

The next fifteen will not be as easy!

SNAKE BITES OF HURT - GRIEF - GUILT

The break of dawn is minutes away. A wintery chill hugs the darkness and yet it is almost May. My headlights show the way as I drive to a very special place where I always visit alone. Thousands know of this place named Pony Pasture. Despite the chill, sleet, or spring time warmth, you will faithfully find me here on this special biblical morning.

It's Easter Sunday and daylight is signaling to the waterfowl it's breakfast time. Flying just inches above the noisy rapids, a pair of geese are fussing over something. An Eagle arrives, perching atop a Sycamore tree, scanning for its first morning feast.

Wearing gloves and hiking shoes, I crawl along the dynamited boulders stacked alongside the southern bank of the James River. I know exactly where this path leads me - to the same granite boulder I have sat upon for the past quarter of a century. Cold to the touch, it has remained steadfast in place, awaiting my Easter morning return.

The gray skies have yielded to a pale blue, with a mix of golden rays arriving behind the river tree line. The roaring rapids captivate my soul with the transformation from darkness to daylight. It commands total awe. Within minutes, the sun's rim peers over the treetops while the river's rapids reflect its radiant glow. Easter's sunrise has risen! Little is written in the manuals of psychology about expressions of thanks. For me, it's a validation of kindness, giving thanks to the professionals, friends, family and God that have walked with me through my darkest of times. Being appreciative is essential because it helped me reach closure. My Easter morning trip to the James is a moment of renewed appreciation for life and all the beauty it gives to living.

A key element in times of peril is not to simply pray for better mental stability — then expect to get well. The key element is to pray for God's gift of courage and to strive to make positive change. My faith fed my motivation to seek that new day. I tapped into his spirit of guidance then traveled his challenging path.

Decades have passed since the 1980's. Those earlier trips to Pony Pasture, lugging the burdensome weight of hurt, grief, and guilt, rode heavily upon my shoulders. Having a good sense of balance and leg strength, I stepped from boulder to boulder to find my seat. Now I share a glorious feeling after decades of hard work. I'm blessed to be free! Throughout this time, my heart and soul have weathered the battles, winning the war to find that inner peace. Mental and physical adjustments resulting from two major surgeries during the Eighties impacted my quality of life. I underwent a Koch pouch removal at the Cleveland Clinic in 2015, then knee replacement in 2018. Considerably frail today, my previous steps across those boulders are now cautious crawls. The blessings bestowed upon me while witnessing the many sunrises are unquestionably worthy of my gratefulness.

My favorite quote by author John Steinbeck, applies to every human on Earth. Edward Sulzbach, a highly respected FBI agent in Richmond's regional office, used this particular quote frequently while lecturing law enforcement officers. Mr. Steinbeck wrote, "There are those amongst us who live in rooms of experience that we can never enter." There were few pictures of joy hanging on my walls. You, the reader of these chapters, can never enter the rooms of my life and feel the ravishing effects of my hurt, grief, and guilt. Nor can I ever enter yours!

My snake bites were devastating. They conquered my soul of existence, creating disruptive and destructive behavior, and sadly I felt my only option was suicide. Humans throughout history have unknowingly allowed this bucket of slush to rot their souls, causing many to take their lives. My bites were debilitating as they dominated every aspect of my personal and professional life. My emotions were stifled at an early age. Opportunity for expression of feelings didn't exist. My rigid childhood upbringing with zero affection, attending church, and the traits that I picked up from the Burley family instilled in me a strong self-conscience. My childhood development of knowing right from wrong was firmly ingrained.

During my career, I arrested thousands of individuals. Many were seasoned criminals who represented total disregard for mankind, with no sense of self- consciousness. They never knew the "Golden Rule" or were taught ethical standards. Many lived a life of emptiness, having little remorse or accountability.

Each of these emotional burdens can be overlapped or be exclusive. Some traumas left me with hurt, while at the same time, grief, and guilt sat upon my shoulders. The greater your conscience the more likely regret lingers nearby.

Accepting responsibility for my actions required a moral strength toward being apologetic to those I hurt. Each domino had check offs that required full court completeness. Each visit, each meeting, and each issue of discussion had to be afforded the right setting. Sincerity and exercising an ability to listen were essential. Taking the time to calmly share feelings with each other and giving the courtesy to respectfully listen makes the healing process rewarding. Shouting and arguing are certainly not options.

The beautiful James River continues to roar and the eagles boldly greet the sunrise, while the granite stones sit timelessly still. Pony Pasture and the James are partners that helped me cleanse my poison of bygone years. The rising sun, roaring waters, and God's grace of healing were effective in that cleansing. Year after year, little by little, my poisonous venom of the burdens of stress and despair became lighter and eventually dissolved, rewarding me with a renewed spirit. That snake is dead. I trust that my boulder will always be there for me. I know the beauty of next year's Easter sunrise will be as radiant as ever.

Flying in tandem, a pair of squawking geese will be fussing over something!

Sixteen to Seven, then Three

The success of rehabilitation, particularly in my case, was the emphasis the psychiatry staff placed upon me to pace my goals. My 43 years of life accumulated many dysfunctional patterns that would demand extensive time to resolve. When I departed the hospital, I had clear acceptance and understanding that I carried decades of slush in the pit of my stomach, and did not expect to quickly flush it all clean and be happy in a few months.

Each day had its priority. Adjustments to my everyday life started at my kitchen table each morning. Many of my issues were heavy weights and demanded months, and even years to conquer. I struggled with the transition from being a police officer to a civilian, from living with my wife and son to an immediate separation. The most important priority was my continued recovery while remaining involved with my toddler-age son. He needed his dad during his crucial years of development. I likewise needed him.

There were no set guidelines I put in place to determine which domino I would tackle next. Multiple dominoes were addressed simultaneously. Many were issues impacting my stability and quality of life that would require months of diligent effort, while others required a different approach to resolve in a quicker time frame. However, there was one exception, and that was turning in my police badge. It was city-owned property, yet it was a part of me.

* * * * * *

I hosted a farewell breakfast in the headquarters cafeteria the morning of my last day on the Police Bureau. As the meal concluded, I stood beside my wife and son, seated next to me at the table, and thanked city officials for their support through my years of illness. Attending were court judges and police chief Colonel Frank S. Duling, accompanied by his majors and command staff. This would sadly be my formal and final goodbye. I had only several hours left in this day to wear my uniform for the last time. Clinging for every moment to keep this day alive, I browsed all through police headquarters, giving farewell hugs and handshakes. Gwen took Nick to the hospital day care then walked nearby to work. Immediately, a surge of emptiness overcame my surroundings as I silently drove home.

I informed Chief Duling that I would turn in my uniforms and equipment in a few days. I requested that I would be allowed to keep the uniform I was wearing because I wanted to be buried in it. I also told him I wanted to turn my badge over to him. The chief knew this would be difficult for me and respected my wish. He responded with a soft voice of kindness.

"Take your time Glen, when you feel like bringing it down to me that will be fine."

My badge remained on my uniform shirt for several months. I was Glen Burley now, a civilian retired from public service. The time had come to relinquish that part of me that I could no longer hold. Turning in my badge was an acceptance of reality.

I went downtown to visit the Chief. Emotions in check, I placed badge #189 in his hand. This was a major moment of healing, and my second domino conquered.

* * * * *

Of my 16 dominoes, the longest in terms of healing and eventually finding peace and forgiveness was the domino earmarked for my father. Here I was researching him and his room of experience in life, and my father had been deceased for 15 years. The early stage of my healing regarding him was what I had learned in therapy. Where was his hatching nest for that anger? My counseling afforded me an ability to acquire some understanding of my dad. I traveled to Amherst and spent hours going around and talking with his friends and natives of the county, inquiring about whom my dad was and how they envisioned him. Their general consensus was the same, "a gentleman, highly regarded, and humble."

Visiting his grave time after time was the ultimate path to healing. I never had to make an appointment. His soul and presence were always there waiting. Years later the time had come when acceptance and forgiveness embraced us as Father and Son. My newfound courage in expressing my thanks to him for being a father whom I believed truly loved me, and to set free my painful memories to the winds, was a validation I had longed for. Dr. Levenson would be proud of me.

* * * * *

When I began attending school, I walked a half-mile to catch bus # 26. About six students of all grades gathered at a fork of two roads at the base of the hollow. As I stood among them, I felt I wasn't the best looking pumpkin in the patch. I was some shy first grader sporting hand-me-down clothing with wide ears and a big nose. This made me an ideal candidate for bullying and intimidation.

One morning at the bus stop an older student named Page Campbell began passing out little squares of Hershey's chocolate candy. He intentionally skipped offering me any. There were giggles as Page continued to pass out additional squares. Obviously, my feelings were hurt. As the school bus came into view, we gathered our books and other belongings. When we were loading the bus, Page handed me a whole chocolate bar. He said it was better than what the other students had eaten.

The Burley Hollow bus stop was the first on the route in the morning and the last in the afternoon. Our ride time to the school was a few minutes past an hour. As we rode along, I was enjoying my chocolate. It had a little different taste, but I ate the entire bar.

All through my years of attending school, mom always saw that we had a hearty breakfast before we departed for school. Hot biscuits, with homemade preserves and fresh milk was a daily. I always enjoyed her oatmeal smothered with fresh butter and local honey. Eggs and bacon were also morning fare.

The bus was full, and we were on the final trek before arriving at the school. Suddenly I felt sick, experiencing unusual stomach cramps. It was frightening especially since other kids kept looking and laughing at me. Then it came. Within seconds my undershorts were saturated with flowing stool. My intestinal system had surrendered not to candy, but to the excessive consumption of a laxative — X-Lax!

Confused and not able to comprehend why this was happening embarrassment crushed me. The bus arrived at school and the students unloaded as if nothing had occurred. Clutching my paper lunch bag I slid down in my seat from view of the bus driver. The more I moved about the more the liquid stool ran down my legs and even into my shoes.

What Page Campbell did was an act of despicable betrayal, causing a young child to suffer emotional damage for the simple rewards of enjoying his trickery and having some giggles, which somehow he felt were funny and cool.

Mr. Austin pulled away with his assumed empty bus. He parked it near the courthouse and walked away. I also was frightened that someone would discover me and accuse me of skipping school. The repeated discharge of stool was overwhelming. My brain was in a fear and flight mode. I unlatched the emergency handle to the rear door and exited the bus. At the age of six, I knew the main street in town, and that it led to the town's traffic circle. Afraid and not knowing how to ask for help I decided to head home — 7 miles away. Leaving a trail of stool along the sidewalk, I arrived at the circle and continued walking West on Rt. 60.

This was around 1948. About a mile west of the circle, mailman Billy Carter pulled over. He quickly observed my unusual situation, and asked for my name. His car was full of mail and boxes preventing any space for me to ride on his seat.

He removed an old burlap bag from his trunk and placed it on the floor board, then helped me crouch down on it. The scent from me was sickening. Mr. Carter stopped at the Sardis Grocery store and requested Knight Hill, the store owner to come out and identify which Burley family I belonged to. In a few minutes Mr. Carter had taken me home. To this day, I remember the exact location on the highway where he pulled over to help me. I will always remember Mr. Carter.

Mom cleaned me up and told me to go lie down. That was the end of that! No complaint was filed and no official at the school was informed. I was thankful that the story got around what Page did to me and peer pressure was placed upon him so that I was off limits. He never bothered me anymore.

"Hello."

"Is this Page Campbell?" I asked.

"Yes, who is this?"

"Glen Burley."

"How in the hell did you find me? That's right you're a cop down in Richmond."

Page's whereabouts had been learned from sources in Amherst. When I called, he was working in Northern Virginia. After some small talk the discussion led to the "X-Lax prank." He claimed not remembering the incident, but listened to my reason for locating him. I emphasized the severity of his cruel act and how it devalued my self esteem. I spoke how this incident was hurtful and altered my trust toward others.

I felt it essential and helpful for me to locate Page and express to him how his actions had impacted my sense of individuality and comfort zone among other school children. Years later, we were attending a funeral home in Amherst. He walked over and greeted me. He called me as he approached, "Glen" — "How the hell are you?" It had been many years. I didn't recognize him. "Hell, you know me — this is old Page Campbell. Man, I'm sorry about that time you messed up your britches."

I accepted his comments as his acknowledgment and apology. We shook hands then we mingled apart. I also will remember Page Campbell.

* * * * *

Some of the most adventurous and dramatic times of my life were serving as an Army paratrooper. We traded gallon-size cans of army mess hall coffee with pilots to take us up for jumps! Wearing jump wings, brass cross pistols and the Screaming Eagle patch on my uniform signified in my mind, I was part of the elite. Pride and confidence sat high upon my shoulders.

Just months before my scheduled discharge, the Company Commander promoted me to Sergeant. Within a few weeks the Captain assigned me to be a squad leader responsible for ten military policemen. It was awesome to wear the green shoulder command bands with "Rendezvous with Destiny" insignia pins over them.

As a new Sergeant and squad leader, if we were not working patrol, we were conducting jumping exercises and intensive combat training. The Vietnam War was beginning to intensify and combative readiness was paramount.

Then came the recruiting team — three highly decorated paratroopers dressed in their Class A's. For a six-year re-enlistment they offered me an immediate promotion to the rank of E-6, or staff Sgt., including a $3000 signing bonus. Earlier I had met with Los Angeles police recruiters visiting the post. After tests and background checks, I was accepted by them and scheduled to be hired pending my discharge and a physical. Edith was pregnant with our second child that was due in the fall. Without question with six years of re-enlistment, I was certainly headed to Vietnam. I remember her holding our son, Douglas, sobbing and pleading to me, not to sign the papers. Her points were valid and persuasive.

She was also successful in convincing me to remain in Virginia. With one child and the second fast approaching, her plea was well taken. I canceled my physical examination with Los Angles Police Department, and shortly thereafter became a police officer with Richmond, Virginia.

The times were exciting. I rented a single room in a boarding house that served hot meals. The reality was amazing. I'm now a rookie, in uniform, with gun and badge, and scheduled to start the police academy in weeks. Edith remained in Lynchburg.

Then came the unexpected — the eye of the Screaming Eagle became tearful. I learned after leaving Fort Campbell that some of my military police company had been deployed to Vietnam. The squad I commanded was part of that deployment. Grief kicked me in the gut when I learned some of my squad members came back home in flag draped coffins or body bags.

Whenever I saw the shoulder patch of the Eagle on Vietnam warriors or heard taps during Veterans Day, it would buckle me over in grief and regret. This painful emotion repeatedly reared its demons inside me every year. I knew after sessions with Dr. Levenson that I had to travel to Washington. Anita accompanied me to the Vietnam Wall. I searched looking for their names, the names of my fellow military policemen that we had patrolled and jumped together at Campbell. All I had to give them was my honor, respect — say "Goodbye" and whisper, "I am sorry." They freed my pain and gave me forgiveness. I let my squad down, and felt I had abandoned them. They went, fought, and gave their life for God and Country — I didn't.

* * * * *

Adolescents do stupid things, often not giving consideration to the consequences that lie within. Dad owned two horses, Coley and Hazel. This pair of working giants were an essential element to our farming. Every piece of farming equipment we owned, they pulled, either individually or in tandem. Farm tractors were not commonplace, nor could our family afford one. I killed Hazel resulting from a despicable act.

It was a rainy day and both horses were in their respective stalls. My cousin had snatched a couple of cigarettes from Uncle Hal, and we headed to the hay barn to smoke'm. I took no joy in emptying my slush bucket when I told this story during therapy. I take less joy in writing it now. After our smokes, I retrieved a can of neat's-foot oil from the harness rack, and he went to fetch a milk stool.

We entered Hazel's stall, lubricated a pitch fork handle with the oil and inserted it into her vaginal tract. Trying to stay balanced on the stool, we continued inserting the handle further, until she reacted. We noticed some blood on the handle and we became frightened and stopped. I cleaned the handle by sliding it across the grass. My cousin opened the barn door, and Hazel exited.

I had difficulty trying to go to sleep that night. Did we injure Hazel? The reality of guilt and fear started to influence my thoughts. Coley and Hazel were always seen together. They were partners in work, just like they were partners in rest, and would be seen in the summer lying together under a shady tree. I remember my Dad would talk to them sometimes. My anxiety lifted a little when I saw them the following day grazing together. I felt a sigh of relief and a self assurance that I wasn't doing that again.

A few days later a renewed anxiety smacked me with a raw sickness. Standing near the barn lot was Coley -- where was Hazel? I learned early on with farm life that death attracts buzzards. Feeling like I was about to vomit, I turned and started scanning skyward. There they were, a thousand feet up, circling and giving nature's indication that dying or death was below.

I went upstairs and changed out of my school clothes. There had been no discussions or inquires about the whereabouts of Hazel. I walked down a slope about a quarter-mile from the barn. There was Hazel -- lying across some decades old path, created by the livestock that lead from the barn to the nearest creek. Joining my guilt and fear was a new emotion — deep sadness.

I told my Mom about the buzzards; she told my Dad. Before sunset, we walked down and took a canvas tarp to cover her. He never spoke. I was afraid to, and silence reigned. I confessed this story to my father during one of our domino talks at his grave.

I still see her face as if I saw her today. She was chestnut tan with a patch of white running from her nostrils up between her eyes. The next day a special truck came and hauled her away. Hazel probably died of internal organ damage likely causing infection, then death. I rode her bareback without a bridle. She was strong, loving, and trusting. She helped my parents make a living – I killed her.

* * * * *

I was in a deep sleep after working the evening shift. My telephone rang at 5 am.

"Glen, this is your Aunt Mae — your home place is on fire, you better git on up here!" I immediately went in combat mode. Two minutes later, I was hauling ass to Amherst. The silence of the tiny towns of Cumberland and Buckingham were disrupted as I barreled through them on Rt. 60, traveling recklessly at high speeds, and driving the straight stretches at one hundred miles per hour. From East Richmond, the 120-mile trip seemed forever. Are my parents alive? Is my brother Sam all right? Was anything saved? Daylight was breaking when I entered the hollow. Still speeding, I rounded a curve, sliding sideways, topping a hill that put me in sight of my home. This beautiful white farmhouse, with its contrasting green tin roof, surrounded by willows and red maples — was gone! All that was left were smoldering timbers, and a towering rock chimney cooling from the intense heat just minutes earlier. Mom and Dad got out safely and were taken up to Uncle William and Aunt Ruby's home. Sam was awakened by the crackling sound of burning rafters. He stood silently in shock as smoke swirled around his eyes. An open family Bible singed from the flames laid upon the front porch steps. A slight breeze flipped its pages facing the heavens.

For my entire youth and into my adulthood, this home was my salvation. It shielded me from times of uncertainly, in times of solitude, and it gave me comfort. My Mickey Mantle and Ty Cobb baseball cards were forever lost. As a little adventurous boy, it even allowed me to pee out my bedroom window onto its back porch roof then watch the little stream trickle toward the roof's edge.

* * * * *

I cannot count the times, nor name the places, where I have responded to scenes of human violence fueled by alcohol or anger, that resulted in death. This also includes investigating vehicle accidents associated with recklessness, speed, and, yes, alcohol. Death seems to always proclaim itself the victor. Suicides are another matter. Working in patrol, I took occasional reports of individuals killing themselves. Responding to suicides demand police officers to exercise unique compassion. The individual may have lived alone, and required the tedious task of locating names of next of kin, then contacting them. Memories of two suicides during my lifetime will never leave me.

"C'mon boy" was my Dad's trademark phrase. No, it wasn't, "Glen, would you like to pal around today with your Dad? or "Son, let's go get a Coke and some peanuts, does that sound good?" Being the oldest son, I was expected to be his tag-a-long sidekick. Wherever he drove his pickup, I was young as four or five years old, riding shotgun, stretching to peek out of the window, or I crawled into the pickup's bed. When I became older, my cousins and I would let the tailgate down and sit on it, swinging our legs over the edge. One summer day, Dad was driving back home from Amherst, and "Jr" and I were enjoying our fun ride with our legs dangling over the tailgate. Dad's top speed on Rt. 60 was usually 30 MPH – maximum! Our laughter and enjoyment abruptly changed when suddenly a Cincinnati-bound Greyhound bus rolled up to just feet behind us. We could see the annoyed bus driver setting up high above us. This Greyhound was now running a little late.

One of his "c'mon boy" trips still lingers like it was yesterday. It was very early this particular morning when we left Burley Hollow. Dad pulled up in front of a two-story farmhouse about three miles away in Woodson Hollow. Like the Burleys, this hollow had the Woodson homeplace and community, with additional homes built later by family members.

Maude Woodson, pronounced "Maudee", was the primary resident of this house. Someone in her family had gotten in touch with my dad for some needed help. Her brother Ernest Woodson had walked outside that morning at the break of daylight, stood beside the lap siding of the house, and blew his head off with a shotgun.

Not aware of why we were there, I followed my dad as we walked from the front around to the side of the house. It was just like any other tag along day — until I looked down. The Sheriff and County Medical Examiner had departed earlier, and Mr. Woodson's body had been taken away. Unexpectedly, I walked up on fresh human blood, in puddles, slowly seeping down into the grass.

Then, I looked up. Towering skyward along the white painted lap boards, up near the upstairs window were small chunks of brain and skull, matted together with hair and blood. Some pieces had fallen back to the ground, forming a little pile along the foundation wall. I was too young to comprehend specifically what had occurred. Nearby, a shotgun was leaning against the house. That wasn't what mattered.

What did matter was being subjected to this visual that to this day I can still see. This was horrific for anyone to witness or experience, especially a child. The adults that stood around in the yard that day were oblivious of my presence. Mr. Woodson committed suicide on his 49th birthday in the fall of 1951. — I was nine.

* * * * *

It was a school day and I was assigned to Patrol Unit 213, a South Richmond beat, working Westover Hills and adjoining communities. Most of the officers were in police or traffic court that morning. Westover Hills was an old, established neighborhood, bordering the James River with large two story brick homes, huge oak trees, and well-groomed lawns. The landscaped hill allowed homeowners to relax on their porches, watching an occasional Bald Eagle snatch a small mouth bass for its chicks.

"Unit 213" comes on the dispatcher.

"213", I acknowledge.

" ..... Dorchester Road — caller would like to see an officer — 10-7" (time)

This type of call could be any number of scenarios.

As I began to ascend the front steps, I noticed a middle-aged lady standing in her front doorway I immediately noticed there was no life in her eyes, her movement subdued. She appeared to be alone, inviting me into the living room. I inquired as to how I could help her. Speaking calmly, she informed me that she thought she heard something fall upstairs.

"Some kind of noise." I think a picture may have fallen off the wall." Her residence was one of these original Westover Hills homes, two stories with large, high ceiling rooms. I questioned her, regarding if any other people were in the house. She indicated she was there alone.

Calm, but vigilant, I began to climb the long stairway. She stood quietly in the hallway. I was well aware that I was alone, and backup units if needed were scarce. So — what do I have here? Has a bird gotten inside the home and knocked over something, a squirrel possibly? Or, do I have an armed criminal who has somehow entered the house with intent to harm this lady? I slowly and quietly climbed.

I paused at the top of the steps, listening for a possible squirrel or bird. I sensed the unusual, yet unexplainable. There was a faint, periodic "splat" coming from one of the bedrooms. My hand on my pistol grips, I eased into the doorway. "Splat."

I glanced up. An instantaneous childhood flash of Woodson Hollow blinded me. I looked into a bedroom, its bed neatly made and its high ceiling, with clinging human brains, skull bits, hair and blood —"Splat".

Now, the toughest moment. I eased around the foot of the bed and witnessed the obvious. Someone had sat on the edge of the bed and placed a shotgun under their chin, and committed a similar suicide as Mr. Woodson's. Flesh was dropping from the ceiling into a pool of blood, surrounding the body.

I closed the bedroom door with dignity, and came downstairs. She was sitting in the kitchen. When I entered, she stood up. I looked her in her eyes, and softly said, "It wasn't a picture frame." I detected she knew that. Kinetic energy coming from a shotgun blast inside a home — she knew.

I called Sgt. Anderson, at Second Precinct to brief him then waited for a detective and the Medical Examiner to meet me. I began writing a police report, sitting with her in the kitchen. This lady was in total shock. It had locked up all her reactions and emotions. It was impossible for me to establish an identity upstairs due to the total facial destruction. It was imperative that I protect the crime scene until the investigators arrived. She asked me to give her a description of the clothes the person was wearing. When I returned from upstairs determining his clothing description, she received a telephone call from a school official who was inquiring about the whereabouts of her son.

The investigation indicated she saw her son leave the house for school, carrying his books about 7:30 a.m. Apparently, unknown to her, he slipped back into the house, entering from an unused door. She showed us his framed school picture, displayed in the den. My memory of his picture, the gut wrenching stress of seeing a faceless young man and the silence in his bedroom broken by the splatter of his falling flesh. This too, I'll never forget. Her son didn't live to celebrate his 16th birthday.

* * * * *

During the earlier years of our marriage, Gwen had expressed her desire to me that we have a child. I remember being adamant against her feelings, because my track record of fathering three children with my first wife, was far from commendable. I simply didn't want to fail in that regard again. This viewpoint was selfish and disrespectful of her wishes. Unfortunately, I didn't think likewise at that time.

Prior to our marriage I had already been diagnosed with ulcerative colitis. During our discussion of having a family, I was taking moderate dosages of drugs to fight the inflammation. It was obvious my health had worsened, and Gwen was working long hours in the emergency room. Simultaneously, she was attending Virginia Commonwealth University at night pursuing her Master's Degree in Nursing Administration.

Years passed, she graduated with honors, my colon was removed, and medications were no longer needed. We had a renewed talk about her wishes. This time, I respectfully honored them. I knew this meant very much to her. She had been an extraordinary wife supporting my medical battles, and a dedicated employee seeking higher ambitions in her profession. She earnestly wished for us to have a child.

This was beginning to get exciting! I had visions of our tiny "Burley smurf" entering this world and arriving home to Glyndon Lane. An infant born of two "Leos'," fighting for territorial rights with two Scottish terriers, would forever change our household. Gwen was a sight to see, eight months pregnant, her hair up in a bun, immaculately dressed, waddling about in MCV.

I stood next to Gwen's bedside at Chippenham Hospital, holding her hand and stroking her hair. She was obviously drowsy, lying there quietly. Complications had developed the day before requiring she seek immediate hospitalization. Her OBGYN physician entered the room. After a few moments of consultation, he asked me if I wanted to see our little son. I nodded that I did. When I started to depart with him Gwen called me back. She looked up at me with teary eyes, "Make sure he has all of his fingers and toes."

I walked with the doctor down a long hospital wing. There were no patient rooms along the way. He stopped at a closed door, placing his hand on my shoulder. "Are you going to be all right?" I indicated that I would. He said he would be near and would wait for me. Positioned in the center of this room was a long table with a stainless steel top. There, alone on this table, sat a stainless steel tray. I eased over and looked down at my nude little guy, laying face up. His purple-greyish skin cleansed and dry. Our one and only moment together was etched in time with silence, a hurtful loss, and why?

Slowly, I delicately lifted his tiny hands and feet, counting all of his fingers and toes. He seemed to be perfect. A surge of helplessness overtook my emotions. He was so close to crawling around, harassing our Scotties. I thought, should we have waited longer and made sure that all residual traces of medicine I took for a decade were clear. My physicians assured me I was fine. It was God's call — for now, it was not to be.

Our sadness and disappointment were compounded by our silence instead of embracing each other's needs. We each grieved our personal trauma. We just did so silently. I made every effort to give her emotional and loving support, especially during the months following our loss.

* * * * *

Dr. Levenson had the unique ability of being able to place me at ease in our therapy sessions. He helped me extract slowly my guilt and shame, allowing the emotional pain to cleanse itself when I shared some of my childhood experiences to him. Exposure to the darkness of farm life were incidents that we saw as children. Witnessing such acts performed by other people created curiosity, and were not questioned. With humble embarrassment and shame, bestiality once lived in Burley Hollow, and the Sardis community. Dr. Levenson provided to me research that this was common, at times in parts of the Appalachian region. That didn't make me less shameful. This sin is written about in the Bible. I prayed to God for his forgiveness.

* * * * *

I didn't learn and realize until years later well into my career as a police officer, that Burley Hollow had a predator, and it wasn't a mountain lion or bobcat. It was a distant relative from another set of Burleys. This larger family than mine lived in a two-story farmhouse near the highway. Everyone walking or riding, traveled by this house to get in or out of the hollow. This family's trademark was growing healthy dark fire-cured tobacco. The tobacco plant peaked at about forty inches in height. It also had a predator — tobacco worms! Eating from the underside of the leaf and difficult to spot, these green, gross looking horned creatures loved to devour tobacco leaves. Perfect tobacco leaves brought top price at auctions. Who best to locate and destroy this enemy — kids. We were shorter, more agile, faster, and had better eyesight than the adults. We were paid well, — a nickel per worm.

This relative was a son of another farming family and eight years my elder. His deceitful actions began with inviting me upstairs to show me his baseball cards. This was fun since he had cards collected long before I started school. I don't remember the player's pictures or their names, but he gave me some. Keep in mind I was around eight years old; he was 16.

As I walked home one day he pulled up driving an old farm truck. He said he had "something" that he wanted to show me. I hopped in and later upstairs we went. He showed me a new silver half-dollar coin, bragging about how neat it would be if I had one.

Nickels and dimes were exciting to have, but a half-dollar would buy me lots of goodies at Sardis store. Then his cunning technique sprang into action.

He unbuttoned his pants and took out his penis, asking me to help him get it hard. This continued by him demonstrating to me how he wanted me to masturbate him. After his pleasures were met, I happily walked home with this big coin in my pocket.

When I look back, as best I can remember, this relative was sly. At times it seemed selective to his choosing, and suddenly he would appear. He knew I walked alone a lot to the highway for little league baseball, or out to the country store. Once he was hunting on our land and approached me inside our hay barn. He removed from his jacket a shiny half-dollar, and handed it to me. Propping his shotgun against the feeder trough, he gestured for me to masturbate him again.

One summer evening, a bad storm hit the hollow. I got caught up in a downpour with intense lightening as I walked home from the highway. I was welcomed inside his home by his Mom until the storm was over. It was suppertime, so I ate supper per her invitation. The next thing I realize, I'm upstairs in this relative's bedroom again. He shows me a larger coin, but he also had a half-dollar coin to compare to the big one. His sales pitch was "that I can buy two times more with the big coin." He gestured to me to hold the heavier coin, a silver dollar, and then he retrieved it.

The storm had subsided, the hollow was darkening, and I wanted to get home. It started the same as in the past. He had spun me into his web of control, pleasure, and sexual abuse. He was ready to take this abuse to another level. He handed me the silver dollar, as I stroked his penis, coaching my head downward, inserting it in my mouth. His sister, brother, and his parents, all were downstairs.

These five or six encounters occurred over a two to three year period. The third oral encounter, and the last, thankfully, was the most disturbing. He lured me into a barn across the creek from the house. We were supposed to gather up curing sticks and tie them in bundles. With the barn door closed, it was pitch dark inside. Just before he closed the door, he reached out to me and said, "Here" It was two silver dollars.

For the first time I felt afraid and intimidated. Like times before, the oral sex began, but this time he suddenly seemed dominant, forceful. His physical control was overpowering and his penis choking me. He was intentionally enjoying himself, at the expense of my fear and discomfort. I found myself in total darkness and frightened with sperm all over my face. That fear was heightened when I had difficulty in the darkness, locating the door to escape.

It was years before I understood the impact that these events had upon me. These raw acts of sexual abuse within the confines of trusting families, while in a respected community, were in the shadows of Sardis Methodist Church. Living a life with feelings of having been violated rots one's self esteem. Unfortunately this demon went into the slush pit as all the others, — the slush pit of silence.

This domino was two parts — the first being discussions with Dr. Levenson and his therapy team dealing with self esteem, healing, and shame. Their in-depth sessions were a high priority, since I had suppressed these experiences for some 30 years. Within two years of release from the psychiatric unit only one thing was left, — the second being confrontation, with a cup of anger!

When I returned to Amherst County to seek election for Sheriff, I took something special with me. Still towering on my bookshelf were only two or three dominos remaining. One still had a pending matter that needed closure and it was earmarked for Burley Hollow. I admit that finishing off this domino wasn't a chapter that I was eager or looked forward to closing. From day one, after returning back home, I carried this domino in my pocket while campaigning. Twice a day I rode by the tobacco barn and where the house once stood. Revisiting memories of 45 years ago flashed to the upstairs and the dark barn — and the relative.

I share a point of psychological disgust: There are sexual abuse stories going back to the 1940's, in this community. An individual is rumored to have sexually assaulted another, and in some cases, assaulted them more than once, constituting acts that warrant felony charges. Yet charges were never filed, victims felt shamed and kept silent, and parents choose not to confront the assailant of their child. What's disgusting is that life goes on in silence and the scars never heal. When I ran for Sheriff it had been 45 years, and how many times had I silently crossed paths with my abuser? A lot of times. That was about to change.

I rolled down out of the mountainous part of the hollow and headed for some vigorous campaigning. The road leveled, entering an area of rich bottom land that once grew that beautiful dark tobacco. Standing amidst a tomato patch was that distant relative. He lived nearby, owned a few cattle and was trying to keep his deceased parent's farmland from growing up in seed pine and broom sage. He waved; I tooted the horn. This was my moment. I pulled over, walked across the creek, and

approached him. We shook hands, leaving the impression
that I had stopped to campaign. I inquired if he had
a couple minutes, and he acknowledged that he did.
Nearby was an abandoned collapsed hog pen. Focusing
on being in control, I started walking away from him
and suggested let's go over here to this old hog pen. He
followed. We straddled over the weathered logs and sat in
opposite corners.

Immediately rising was a surge of emotions,
exactly like in the hospital room when I told the doctor
that I was "just Glen Burley." The same when I told my
deceased father at his grave about the times I missed our
father-son bond, or when his scornful anger belittled me.
Trembling and sobbing, I knew exactly what I wanted to
say – it was just too painful to say it.

"I can still feel your dick in my mouth." These
were my first struggling words that I said to him. He
sat sheepishly while I expressed empathically that what
he did to me hurt me. He hurt me in the physical sense
also. I told him that his trickery undermined my trust
and violated all human decencies of me early in my
childhood. I further stated that as a police officer in
training sessions I learned about sexual abusers such as
him and that my development of anger and hate toward
him had manifested over time.

He quietly sat fifteen few away, humbled and in
tears. He painted a picture of his childhood and being
subjected to inappropriate experiences in his home.

His demeanor was contrite, expressing to me a
sincere apology for his conduct.

I was 53, — he was 61. I stood up, and he did
likewise. I walked across the hog pen, and shook his

hand, and expressed my forgiveness. He reiterated feeling sorrow for his actions. As we returned to his tomato patch, he seemed broken by my visit. The breeze had dried up our tears. Burleys grew up seldom getting hugs — I gave him one!

The visit with him was a journey long overdue. I had reached the summit of Mt. Everest. It was, as expected emotionally draining, but I hit all the targets of healing in my first words spoken to him. He stood and watched me as I entered my car. We waved, and off I drove. My next stop wasn't in Amherst, shaking hands and politicking – it was a few hundred yards down from the tomato patch.

I pulled over adjacent to a vehicle-size boulder rising above the road embankment. Standing on this boulder, I looked across a hay field, divided by Possum creek — the same two fields that once grew that rich green tobacco, yielding fat tobacco worms that netted me a nickel bounty per worm. This domino in my pocket had become my sidekick, kinda like my pocket knife. It was time for us to part ways. I held it in my hand, and thought about the momentous achievement that was just accomplished. I pitched it hard and watched its path as it sailed across the creek. As you know, I didn't win the election for sheriff, but this day, in Burley Hollow, I won the election for acceptance, the election for finding peace, and most important, I had a landslide victory for forgiveness.

* * * * *

My son, Nicholas caused me to realize ten years after my hospitalization, that I overlooked a domino missing from my list. At 13, he revealed to me an appreciation for nature's life and compassion that didn't exist much when I was at his age.

With tears in his eyes, and six words spoken, he staggered me when we went arrow hunting on my homeplace. Nick always found traveling to Amherst a childhood treat. He loved hanging out with Grandma Burley, and like his dad, he enjoyed all of her homemade sweets. It amazed him how it appeared to him that the sky and stars at night were much closer to earth in Burley Hollow than in Richmond. The open space of mountains and hay fields were a different world to him than in suburban Henrico County.

When Nick was 12, I gave him a .22 Browning rifle. I had more enthusiasm for him having a rifle than he did. Baseball was his niche, not so much hunting. I took it with us to Amherst to shoot. Arrow collecting was a big thing among his classmates. He wanted to search for arrows, and I wanted to try out his new rifle.

We were walking along an abandoned path, once active a hundred years ago when relatives visited each other over the mountain. I heard a little chickadee chirping on a tree limb above me. This was my chance to test the accuracy of Nick's new rifle. Nick's attention was directed on finding arrows and he didn't notice what I was about to do. Pow! The crack of the rifle shot startled him. Fallen at our feet was this dead little bird. I picked it up to see where the bullet entered, observing blood on its soft chest feathers. I thought, "Not bad for the first shot from a new gun." Nick had a different and hurtful reaction. "Dad!" "Why did you do that?" Taking the bird from my hand, his eyes tearing up, it quickly was realized that I had made a terrible mistake.

His sadness that I killed this beautiful creature and his look of compassion for this chickadee were so impacting it left me feeling inept. Two cultures had just clashed.

Here was my son who learned early on to love all creatures, snakes included, questioning how I could be so nonchalant with killing this bird, especially with his rifle!

In our days of childhood when we neared the age to hunt wildlife, we constantly shot birds on the farm. The smaller the bird, the better our marksmanship. Three birds were off limits — the Cardinal, which is our state bird, Robins, too welcomed in springtime, and Dad's Baltimore Orioles.

That incident made me reflect on my childhood culture, and how we came up short in respecting nature's creatures. I profusely apologized to Nicholas that afternoon, and more times later. He accepted that my action was not malice, simply wrong. Some parental guidance years ago may have saved many birds their life also.

Since my knee replacement, I have returned to that path, and stood by the tree that the chickadee fell from. I prayed to God to forgive me for that act I committed in front of Nick, but for all the birds that I killed growing up on the farm. God's forgiveness and Nick's compassion were teaching moments. What I did was profoundly wrong.

* * * * *

At my graveside service, a distant sound of taps will someday echo across a cemetery, signaling the final chapter in my book of life. My last domino will most likely still be standing on my book shelf. Many aspects of this domino have been addressed and conquered, but unlike all the others, acceptance and interest are far reaching. My sons, Douglas Anthony and Donald Ray, both in their 50's, are my last domino.

My realistic conclusion comes from a saying, "You only get out of something what you put into it," My investments in them, at crucial times in their youthful life was, sadly to say, practically zero! I experienced a romantic lure and excitement of a new relationship with a lady far different in class and poise than I ever knew. Most everything centered around her, to whom I eventually married. My new wife's interest in their well being, urged me to go to Lynchburg frequently and we would take them shopping for new clothes. Dorrie loved Gwen when she came to town and took Dorrie shopping for nice clothes. When Edith and I became divorced, I gained legal custody of our three children, and they lived with their two grandmothers.

My sons' pain of mental abandonment and yearning for fathership were cheated from their childhood. They felt less worthy because in their eyes, my priorities didn't include them. My punishment today is their absence in my life. Yet, more painful for them was, and probably still is, was my absence in theirs. That void remains stagnant and still lingers.

Genuine, sincere, and repeated efforts for conciliatory progress have been made at different times to each of my sons. They live in Lynchburg, Virginia, near their sister. They each have been wounded by us as parents. They were devalued. They were left feeling insignificant, and were subjected to abuse and neglect more than we will ever know.

I would very much like to die in peace with Doug and Donald. It's likewise important for them that they die in peace with me. They both have children, and Doug has grandchildren. Dorrie, for years has been the "bond maker," hoping to get all of us together for Thanksgiving or travel to Powhatan and meet during Nick's visit from Florida. Dorrie is my unique little girl and promotes family. Now, she's a seasoned professional, distinctively different from her "boys".

For unexplainable reasons the sons chose not to establish a father-son relationship. They are polite, seem respectful, but act hesitant to take any additional steps for a continuous relationship. Our situation is unfortunate, and I reluctantly accept things as they wish them to be. But I don't like it. I trust they know and believe that I love them and that I care for their well being and happiness in life.

I pray that when the taps break the silence at my funeral, that my one remaining domino will have fallen by then. I hold tight a vision that, in due time, the three of us will find a special place to sail it into the winds of healing, forgiveness, and acceptance. It's a possibility to believe that I'm not sure they even know how to love me. I've always hoped they would make the effort and try. It would be an investment for them to experience a quality of life to know and interact with their remaining parent. Our father-son void is far more doable to resolve while living than visiting graves decades later. I pray that they seek the simplistic beauty of peace and hopefully enjoy our remaining years with genuine congeniality, laughter, and family rather than subject themselves to the raw emotions of regret and grief — as I did with my Dad.

SEXUAL DYSFUNCTIONALITY

Built in the 1800's, Sardis Methodist Church was our community place of worship. I remember its magnificent white structure and towering smokestack. Its front doors always unlocked, the church sat in silence except on Sundays. Mr. Andrew Floyd and my dad volunteered there for years, keeping the church grounds and the nearby cemetery in pristine condition. On a warm Sunday, the church windows were opened and the members could be heard singing their favorite gospel songs. Everyone knew each other, and most in the congregation were family.

Pristine church grounds and gospel songs that praised God on Sunday in this serene environment were not all that they appeared to be. I reflect back to those times and see evidence of dysfunctional characteristics in many of the Burley households where sexual inappropriateness was ignored. Families with limited education and fractured communication skills allowed deviate tendencies to be kept secret and accepted. In fairness, I believe it was an ignorance of respectability.

Some of my male classmates at Amherst County High wore their badge of masculinity by carrying a "gold seal rubber" (condom) in their billfold. To show off this masculinity on a Saturday night date, they whipped it out to buy something and revealed the indentation of the condom against the leather. This act in the presence of their peers, was a proclamation — "look at me; I'm gettin' some!"

A marriage occasionally occurred in Amherst County between very distant and sometimes not so distant relatives. Two "sets" of Burleys who lived in the same hollow celebrated a marriage between cousins bearing the same last name. These two kinfolk grew up in sight of each other, played together as kids, rode the same school bus, and attended Sardis Church. My brother's daughter just recently celebrated her second marriage — to another Burley. Like the other cousins, again, they are from different "sets", but still Burley descendants from past generations. When I divorced my first wife, she eventually married a distant cousin of mine, Mr. Scott Burley Jr., who never lived in Burley Hollow.

My sexual awareness did not derive from parental discussions. Dad once gave me a short barn lot analogy on sex. Nothing was taught regarding this topic in the schools during the 1950's. In a gist, he implied, "that if I messed with girls when too young, my pecker would stop growing." Preteen boys learned about sex from older teenagers and most of it was delinquent and some of it was purely disgusting. Personal boundaries were not considered in the rural community by the males toward females as it was in the town of Amherst and suburban Madison Heights. Miles from nowhere, some of my sexual misguidance was influenced by high school farm boys as well as cousins, and male adults. The country teenage boys had a saying around school, "If you ain't thinkin' bout huntin', pickups, and gettin' some — you ain't thinkin'!" Romantic relationships or marriages are severely compromised when unhealthy sexual practices poison the beauty of intercourse.

The alliance with a young son and his dad was generally closer in the farming communities. The young, strong boys were essential at times, requiring an extra pair of hands. Due to the nature of this tradition, mothers were often more disconnected from their sons. This was especially true when compared to relationships between sons and their fathers, during extended periods together in the fields and around the barns. This lifestyle allowed inappropriate sexual tendencies to alter a young gentleman's way of thinking. If some topic wasn't taught as inappropriate, it was assumed to be acceptable.

Our farm was the only farm in the upper hollow that had a bull. Dad owned a small herd of Black Angus cattle for raising and selling spring calves. For additional income, our family always kept two or three milk cows that also delivered calves and provided gallons of milk daily. My aunts and uncles kept milk cows only. During the late summer months when the breeding season began, Dad's siblings would tie a rope around each of their cow's necks and lead them to our barn lot for "servicing." This adventurous annual trip for the milk cow to become impregnated required her to walk about a mile, all downhill, and then return back up the mountain. By now, her mating partner had found the shady side of our barn and was quietly resting, awaiting his next visitor.

This scene was all too common, where two or three old farmers, and on occasion an aunt, stood around, with some leaning over the gate, their arms folded, witnessing livestock mating. This practice was not only deemed acceptable but also seemed entertaining. To most, this would not be considered the norm and frankly distasteful. One might beg the question, "Where are the children during these milk cow visits?" Well, these curious rascals, yours truly included, usually snuck down toward the back side of the barn, climbed up and hid in the hay loft, peaking through the barn logs. This was our bicycle, our Hop scotch, and our skateboard. Sadly — this was our life.

Farm animals mating have been a common reality for thousands of years. Discretion applied by responsible adults is crucial when children are nearby. Sharing information appropriately with your children regarding reproduction and breeding practices can create a proper perspective, preventing negative and dysfunctional habits. This was an experience and lessons learned, despite the nature of my awkward upbringing.

Highlights in Blue

My first apprehension as a Richmond police officer was a female prostitute — actually, there were four, and I hadn't even started in the police academy. The Police Bureau's vice squad was frustrated with their previous attempts to arrest "Madam Hortense" an older lady confined to a wheelchair. She ran a sophisticated brothel from her second floor apartment near City Hall. Many of the veteran police officials knew Hortense and the word on the street was, — "Her "girls" were nice!"

What made the vice squad lieutenant think this rookie could infiltrate her operation when all efforts previously had failed? It appeared he trusted my confidence. This was certainly a new thing for me, but I considered it no big deal and wasn't intimidated. During our pre-raid discussion, I suggested the squad carry out this next raid differently. My idea surprised them. Switch the raid time from evening hours to 7:00 a.m. in the morning.

"What the hell are you talking about?" yelled Lt. Baughan.

I suggested my strategy and how to make this raid a success. They listened.

It was 7 a.m. — on a Saturday morning, and the vice squad members were all in their assigned positions.

I arrived at the apartment driving my 1956 Ford, tan and white, with a green left front fender. My car bore Tennessee state tags, sporting loud mufflers, and the radio blasting rock and roll music. I intentionally let the girls know some fool was in their alley! A lady answered the door sitting in a wheelchair. Greeting her as "Mrs. Hortense", I quickly took charge of the dialogue by apologizing for disturbing her so early.

My ploy was that I was in town on furlough from airborne jump school and my uncle told me about her. Hortense said the girls were still asleep and she was about to make some coffee, and asked if I would like some. I replied, "Sure!" and within moments an attractive lady entered the kitchen, wearing a robe, stretching her arms from her night's rest. To kill any suspicions that Hortense might have. I invited the lady to get dressed and ride up Broad Street to buy some Krispy Kreme doughnuts for everyone. Game on!

I followed her down the back stairway, and I knew the squad had binoculars on us. By now they were freaking out as we roared off, heading west on Broad Street. I was not electronically wired and did not have any communication equipment on me; therefore, I was on my own. I learned later they put a tail on me to see where the hell we were heading. The squad Lt. calmed down once they learned we were returning downtown with a box of hot doughnuts!

While Hortense, my Krispy Kreme lady, and I were having small talk, three additional ladies joined us, some dressed, but one still in her night gown. The vice squad had lost total control and was under duress with the unknown. I was supposed to promptly go upstairs and "make the buy," then signal them to swoop in and make arrests. No, I was still sipping coffee and enjoying doughnuts with Hortense and her four prostitutes — an hour later.

Now the serious business was at hand. Sexual options and a price was agreed upon and money was exchanged. Unknown to me, the arrest could have been made at that moment. Somehow, I forgot to remember that key piece of information during the pre-raid briefing. Naming a price for sexual services and receiving of payment for said services, is sufficient to make an arrest. A legal point in this raid was that Hortense offered me a choice of selecting which prostitute to have sex with; therefore, she and all four girls were subject to apprehension.

The minutes continued to click away — still, no signal. I selected "Ivy Jane" as my sex partner. We had hit it off during our Krispy Kreme run. We walked to her bedroom and began to undress. Standing naked, wearing only my socks, I asked her if I could go in the bathroom and freshen my mouth with some tooth paste. She nodded with approval. I carried my pants with me so I could retrieve my badge and whistle and place them in my socks. When I returned, she was naked, under the covers. I slid in beside her. This moment had my heart racing, seeing Ivy Jane's fantastic body. Despite this, I knew I was about to display my police badge in her face. After about 30 seconds of kissing and foreplay, I nervously reached down in my sock and pulled out my badge and advised she was under arrest. Immediately – I gave the signal —I blew my whistle loudly and repeatedly!

All hell broke loose! The seven member vice squad started kicking in Hortense's back door. Detectives started crawling through a window they completely had smashed out, allowing them to enter our bedroom. I could hear Hortense raging from another room. Ivy Jane grabbed a pillow and threw it, striking me in the face. By now — everyone was pissed!

Someone radioed for the patrol wagon. Soon after its arrival, it departed hauling four unhappy ladies downtown to our police lockup. Rather than deal with medical challenges and logistics taking Hortense down a long flight of stairs, the Lieutenant opted to have the Magistrate respond from police headquarters to the apartment. I swore under an oath before him, attesting to the charges, the magistrate's hand written warrants were served, and Hortense was fingerprinted and released on a bond until her court date.

The vice lieutenant in-charge, and his veteran officers were ecstatic. They had been wanting to bust Hortense for years. They were stressed primarily with concern for my safety, yet reluctantly trusting my judgment. Some comfort existed among them as they had knowledge of me recently being discharged as a military policeman. This raid was written in history as the longest and most accomplished. This was a first — sending a rookie officer into a whore house, to make a buy for sex, and moments later I was speeding off to get doughnuts — with a prostitute!

* * * * *

The "warrant car" was a unit that one officer was assigned. The officer had one mission — to track down individuals who had outstanding warrants for their arrest. This stack of warrants, usually stuck above the sun visor, had worn and curled corners, and most were written months, even years earlier. Individuals named on these papers were excellent at outsmarting police officers, avoiding apprehension at all cost. One day, the officer assigned to this car went on vacation and I offered to work the unit. Sure enough, there was a two-inch stack of warrants tucked over the visor, held together with several dirty rubber bands. Each warrant had a slip of paper stapled to it, recording each time the warrant was tried.

As I browsed through them, one in particular caught my attention. It was old, dirty, and had several "log slips" attached to it. The slips recorded two things, the date tried and the officer's initials. There were little notes on the back side of this warrant — "wanted by Dinwiddie"- "notify state police" - "k-9 used, no luck." His police mug shot was folded inside. The log slips indicated this warrant had been tried numerous times by a lot of officers over a long period of time.

The addresses I tried during that shift resulted in a couple of warrants being served. I knew the mother of one felon named on some capias. After my phone call to her, she met me at Headquarters and pressured him to surrender. This other old warrant became challenging and intrigued me. I waited until we were on the midnight shift and daylight was breaking from darkness on a Sunday morning. We were on Church Hill and it was a great time to strike! With fellow officers in the rear and front surrounding the house, two of us entered. This was my first time there.

We knocked loudly and someone allowed us inside. Everyone seemed nice and knew the drill. Two of us, walking in tandem, searched slowly and thoroughly.

No luck and another entry on the log slip. The illusive fugitive had beaten us once more.

The warrant car officer returned from vacation. We met at headquarters and I questioned him about this particular warrant on North 28th Street. He was as perplexed as we all were. On more than one occasion, he had what he thought was reliable information that this wanted individual was inside this house. Every time the warrant was tried — no luck.

This raggedly looking warrant continued to haunt me. Days later, as I patrolled throughout Fulton Bottom, I wondered what we were missing. Reliable information from the street suggested this sought-after felon was still on Church Hill.

Weeks later, my return visit to this North 28th street address would be un-expectantly different. Again, it was in the wee hours of the morning, about 4 a.m.

Officers surrounded the house, and this time a patrol Sergeant tagged along. We were assisted, per my request, to have a fireman bring in a heavy duty illumination light. We thought we might find a trap door or some giveaway trace leading to his place of hiding.

Slowly like before, room by room, the search was underway. This time we paused and studied each room. Officers do not normally carry a riot stick during a house search. For some unexplainable gut feeling, I had grabbed mine from the trunk.

There we were, fellow police officer R. B. Smith, the city fireman, and myself standing in a dimly lit, filthy, smelly bathroom. A patrol Sgt. was observing us from the doorway. Four of us, standing, looking and studying each wall and crevice — with the fireman blinding us as he aimed his light across the walls. Just inches from our feet was a full length bath tub. A casual glance indicated no more than a bath tub, almost full of dirty clothes. The bathtub curtain was pulled back halfway.

That gut feeling to take my riot stick with me was just confirmed. Quietly signaling my alert and pointing toward the tub, I motioned to the fireman to switch places with the sergeant. Smith slowly pulled the curtain to be fully open. The Sgt. radioed to the units outside, "All units' standby."

My gut told me we had a hit! I took my 36-inch stick and held it firmly with both hands on one end and leaned over a little — jabbing it forcefully downward into the pile of cloths. A split second later clothes start flying into the air. A small Black male bolted out of the tub and was immediately overpowered and handcuffed. The tense fireman, dropped his light with a startled look — "Holy Shit!"

* * * * *

Certainly not as dramatic as the previous experiences, my next enlightening moment will be remembered by many for decades and beyond. "Police Community Relations," also referenced "Community Policing" were new approaches initiated by cities in America during the 1980's. It was a basic and effective approach to unite in a professional and harmonious manner the law enforcement element with neighborhoods having less than admirable concern for law enforcement.

My first assigned patrol beat was Unit 611, the most Eastern section of the City. Half of my beat was on

Fulton Hill, a 100% white neighborhood, and the other half was Fulton Bottom, a 100% black community with close-knit families. These families lived in small framed homes built only feet apart. Regardless of the officers race, not every policeman could work the "Bottom." If the folks in the Bottom didn't like a new beat officer, give him a month and he was gone. I worked 611 for four years.

What occurred in Fulton Bottom during that spring afternoon in 1967, a decade before "community policing," was unprecedented. This simple act of embracing this totally black neighborhood was considered by me and them also, to be exceptional. I believe that during the 1960's, I was a pioneer of good will and professionalism in the poorest and blackest streets of Richmond.

The vacant lot on Louisiana Street was full of kids playing dirt lot baseball. I pulled up in my police car, parked along the first base area, turned my radio volume up high and proceeded to interact with the kids. This was an awesome moment for these kids. It was an awesome moment for me too. They wanted me to hit them some fly balls. The boys gathered in the outfield while an older teenager tossed me pitches to hit out to them. That's how I rolled! The merchants and street dudes called me "Burley," or my street name, "The Hawk." This scene might have looked rare in other parts of Richmond and the Nation, but not in the heart of the "Bottom" on Louisiana Street. The best and most memorable years of my career were my first beat assignment lasting years. I built a priceless trust and respect between the poorest of the poor, the blackest of the black, and this skinny, white patrolman who grew up in the mountains of Amherst, Virginia.

In March 1967, Richmond police officer Glenwood Burley took a moment away from his patrol work to play baseball with youths in the Fulton neighborhood.

Someone called the *Richmond Times-Dispatch* that afternoon, reporting that a policeman was down on Louisiana Street hitting baseballs to the kids. His car was said to be in a field with all its doors open. I was informed the next morning that my picture was on the front page of the newspaper, swinging a baseball bat. That picture was reprinted in 2018 as an archive photo from the *Times-Dispatch*.

Where are the boys? Grown men, fathers, grandfathers, professionals, maybe deceased or in confinement, possibly homeless --- where are they now? It would be a milestone reunion if we could all reunite and embrace our memories of that day! Fulton Bottom's original homes, Louisiana Street, and the vacant lot no longer exist for us to visit and reminisce the crack of the bat and racing to catch my line drive.

Fifty years — year after year, they click away. Then, after decades, a moment of joy jumps up in front of me from nowhere.

"Hawk!" someone hollers.

I turn around and a black gentleman leaving Home Depot approaches me.

"Aren't you Mr. Burley?" he inquires.

"Yeah!" I replied. We talked old times, shook hands, and went about our ways.

This Fulton Bottom kid, now in his sixties, remembered me. He wasn't one of the baseball boys, but he remembered me. Why? It was his trust and respect that I had earned decades ago when I pioneered community policing and my hair was black.

* * * * *

In the 70's and early 80's, our city police officers were struggling with low morale, due to lower salaries and benefits less than those in surrounding counties.

A policeman or fireman could be hired at 21 years of age, and then required to work until the age of 60 before being eligible for retirement benefits. Veteran officers working patrol beats at 53 or 57 years old had long felt downtrodden.

During this same period, a second underlying factor seemed to suppress the everyday enthusiasm of our police officers. It was our unappealing two tone taupe and chocolate uniform. However, despite our lack of love for the colors, the rank and file exercised their pride in neatly wearing them. I remember once during roll call inspection, the sergeant noticed that I was wearing black socks instead of dark brown. He sent me home to change socks!

During the 1800's and continuing up to 1940's, the Richmond Police Department wore the traditional blue uniform. In 1947 some squirrel brain decided to switch from blue to brown. The 1980's were a time for major transformation. Law enforcement in America was well established in becoming a professional public service. Long needed equipment was allocated in budgets. Most police departments were reaching full strength. As far as morale among Richmond officers –- the needle had not moved. A celebrated and transformational day in our City of Richmond was May 15th, 1984. It also was National Peace Officers Memorial Day, a day we give memory, honor, and appreciation for the thousands of law enforcement officers who have sacrificed their lives serving our Nation. For years, our ceremony paying respect to our Richmond fallen officers started with a police/public memorial breakfast in the John Marshall Hotel. After breakfast, the rank and file officers came outside and assembled in marching columns on 5th Street. We marched several blocks to Centenary United Methodist Church for our police memorial service. For many years we marched to St. Paul's Episcopal Church, after the breakfast.

Our march this day — was history! It was our ultimate march of pride, honor, and sacrifice. The police Major's command, "Attention — Forward March" was louder than ever. Our steps were crisp, our chests arched firm, and our heads held high. After three and a half decades, wearing brown — we were marching in blue yet again!

Instantly, an uplifting of morale was evident in every officer on the Police Bureau. This long awaited change was unanimously embraced by the community. We were considered one the best dressed police agencies in the Commonwealth of Virginia.

Damn! — we looked sharp.

A New Day

Thirty-five years ago my life was undergoing transformational experiences. Going from a disability retirement, a planned suicide, surrendering my police badge, psychiatric hospitalization, and a shattered marriage to accepting that life can prevail toward a victorious future was a difficult process.

In these past years I pondered, "what if?" — what if Gwen had not called Captain Bennett? — What if tomorrow was too late? — What if I had injected the deadly syringe? What if Nicholas had grown up without a father in his life? What if I had not witnessed my impressive daughter, Dorrie, receive two degrees, a Bachelor's of Science and Masters of Education at the University of Lynchburg? I am truly thankful and blessed that these "what ifs" didn't come to fruition.

Captain Shook was correct thirty-five years ago when he said to me that I was at high noon in my life. I disagreed then, believing that my life was at sunset, approaching darkness. I was wrong. Amazingly, only a few months ago I began drafting a 15-chapter manuscript. I'm writing my last chapter — a chapter describing these past years of my life as totally uplifting and one of a phenomenal journey.

With prayer, support, and personal commitment, God gave me a new day. He blessed me with a new life.

We sealed the vault of darkness so that it shall never darken my sunshine of this victorious moment. After forty years of life, God taught me it was all right to cry, and it was all right to say, "I love you." I no longer feel shadowed and shamed because I rode hard to conquer individuality and confidence. I have that now, and I ride high, with purpose, pride, and validation, something Richmond police chief Alfred Durham helped me to acquire.

I look back to the 80's and define myself as the old Winesap apple tree, standing alone in a once vibrant orchard. Most of me was dead limbs, bare of foliage, decaying from the trunk and empty of life. Struggling for survival was my one living branch, with a few green leaves and a small cluster of apples. Trim away the dead, nourish its tree roots, give it some love, and this tree will sprout new limbs and be productive, living again with a renewed purpose. That's me!

My highest reward for living was the beauty of reliving my childhood through my son Nicholas. Equally rewarding were the blessings to being a part in his everyday life growing up. I rarely missed a practice or a baseball game during his years playing with the Tuckahoe Little League teams. He always had his dad, when I only had the three steps at my front porch.

I prayed earnestly to God to please keep me in his life. That prayer and many of my others were answered. For the many failures of earlier years, another great opportunity was given to me — *I became a better Father!* My failures and short comings with my first three children were lessons later learned and painfully accepted.

Gwen found my severe mental and medical baggage, and plans of suicide to be too difficult for her to remain in a stable marriage. It was a hill too high to climb. She experienced overwhelming stress and fears of uncertainty and possibly believed her administrative nursing career could be impacted if she remained in the marriage. She moved into an apartment, and I purchased her half of our estate and remain today living in our first home. Our divorce was finalized in 1988. Gwen continued her nursing career and moved to Missouri, and currently resides in Miami. She never remarried.

Immediately upon retirement, I was sought after to work security assignments with numerous agencies. In order to keep my home, I obtained a home equity loan, so monthly payments demanded I work, doing something. The next fifteen years I worked part time positions as a security officer for several large companies. Most of my years were at Phillip Morris USA, and St. Mary's Hospital. My work availability was determined by priority given to my time spent with Nicholas. Our weekends together were never compromised.

Surrendering my badge and accepting that my marriage was dying surely burned holes in my socks. However, it was refreshing to know I still had feet! My first smidgin of renewed esteem occurred when I gave Ms. Anita L. Turner a long stemmed red rose, tucked inside a Ukrop's grocery bag. Anita and I met while attending a Chesterfield County-sponsored divorce workshop. Both of us, raw from emotional meltdowns, presented ourselves nervously to the other as damaged goods. My single rose for her triggered her heart, and hiding it inside a grocery bag triggered her laughter, a laughter she had lost. Our pheromones came alive.

An excellent dresser, classy, and attractive with professional character, Ms. Turner was significant, especially to my rehabilitation, during the first years of our committed and respected relationship. Her reinforcement assured me that I could grow from a damaged past and a divorce to find happiness. With her I did. Our individual experiences had shattered our self worth. I made every concentrated effort to reinforce her validation, values and my admiration for her.

Our fifteen years together were some of my best. Valentine's Day was her most romantic holiday. She would occasionally claim that I was her soul mate. Despite our love and compatibility, one issue seemed to hinder our future together. I was more committed and loyal to Nicholas than I was to our relationship. While she respected our father-son bond, it wasn't to her liking. She preferred 100% of me, but I declined to sacrifice special moments with my son.

Later, Anita retired from Catholic Charities and moved down South to be near her family. We shared many years of enjoyable togetherness and times of excitement. She shared with me her heart to listen. She shared that same heart to love and gave me untold elevations of support and enjoyment. I miss seeing her.

Once a paratrooper, I knew the value of staying in excellent shape. Running gave me an opportunity to ponder the many thoughts that passed through my brain each day. I recorded specific music related to memories of times past and some for just running, enjoying the tempo. My first accomplished *Richmond Times-Dispatch* five-miler was the following fall after hospitalization. Something very meaningful happened to me that morning. Gwen brought Nick downtown to watch me start the race. Training each summer and preparing for the annual marathon event enhanced my mental rehabilitation. Willow Oaks Country Club extended to me a professional courtesy, per member Judge J. Alvernon Smith, allowing me to train on their beautiful golf course. My running occurred at the break of dawn or during the night hours. I proudly hold certificates listing seventeen consecutive dates and recorded times, running the file-milers with a single 10-K race as well. Nick, at the age of thirteen, highlighted the 1995 five-miler by running with me. He whizzed by me going through Monroe Park, but surprisingly I caught up to him near the finish line. He had run hard and was slowing a bit. I held back behind him until we were a few yards from the screaming crowd at the finish line. I made a bold move, passing him, and beating his time by about five seconds. A classic father-son moment!

My desire to maintain a law enforcement connection was established, also, shortly after hospitalization. In my Cornerstone chapter, I wrote about Capt. Tom Clark and his role in my participation with the Central Chapter – Virginia State Crime Clinic, of which I served as President. Eventually, my involvement and leadership were elevated as state chairman of the annual conference on "Terrorism." During 2002, I served our Virginia State Crime Clinic, as 1st Vice President.

These rewarding years of leadership, fellowship, and networking with police officers throughout the Commonwealth were contributing factors to my renewed stability and enthusiasm serving the Crime Clinic. It's always a delight to travel throughout our State, and cross paths with a retired trooper or sheriff you attended the conferences with. My Richmond Police "Retired Patrolman" badge had established its right to fit nicely in my billfold!

I continued to be active after many years, serving on committees, assisting the president and members with our F.O. P. John Marshall Lodge, and the Richmond Retired Police Officers Association. Active participation with peer retirees is rewarding and provides a sense of belonging. If nothing else, attend the meetings occasionally and certainly attend the annual reunion and Christmas party. We are at a moment in our lives that one might see a fellow retiree at a monthly meeting and attend his funeral the following week.

In the summer of 1995, a political race for Amherst County's Sheriff made National news. In this mostly rural community of approximately 22,000 registered voters, six candidates had announced their intentions to run. Of the six, only three had law enforcement experience. A lure to return back home and also the possibility to be Sheriff was too much. After a long conversation with my son and others, their support for my decision to run for sheriff was unanimous. I moved into my mother's vacant home as she had recently entered the town nursing home. In May, days before the filing deadline, I surprisingly announced myself as the seventh candidate. Three more joined in the campaign within a week after my announcement, totaling ten! I was running against a Captain, the Sheriff's chief deputy, a deputy sergeant, a town detective, the county dog warden, a barber, an automotive mechanic, and some kid off the coast of California who was enlisted in the Navy. What a circus! When a candidate placed his campaign sign on the highway, another candidate came along and placed theirs in front of it. In some incidents signs were vandalized or stolen. It got nasty.

I publicly named God as "my campaign manager." Maybe I should have confided with him more on this decision. The voting results were tallied, and I came in fourth. I felt that I was the most qualified. If I had moved back to Amherst a couple years earlier and was the first to announce my candidacy. I might have had a better chance of being elected Sheriff. It wasn't meant to be, and I returned to Richmond.

Beginning around first grade Nicholas began showing interest in foods. During one weekend he asked me for permission to make "squirrel soup" in the bird bath. I answered "sure," and the fun started. Within minutes, Nick was standing on a step ladder gathering up all the old cooking spices his mom had left in the cupboard. Next went my catnip, milk, and mayonnaise. Lunch was served!

All of these ingredients, and more — he had mixed together in the bird bath to feed the squirrels. He told this hilarious story years later to the Chef instructors while he attended school at Le Cordon Bleu College of Culinary Arts.

To make Nicholas' dream become a reality and financially possible, I started a unique and much needed enterprise in Richmond. We named it Mailboxes & Posts — Designs by Nick & Dad. We designed eleven post models, giving each a name. Some names were: "Foolishness," "Willis," "Edward," "Rex." I designed a post in honor of my father, "My Dad," and another I named "Mr. Higgins Esquire" inspired by Harold Higgins, the man who taught me perfection and carpentry in high school. Fifteen years working alone, I traveled throughout Richmond and nearby counties, including Florida digging thousands of holes, installing posts and mailboxes, functioning with very little intestinal tract. This fact confirms the amazing adaptability of the human body. Mailboxes & Posts was absolutely rewarding as I continued to meet new people and serve them, much like I did as a police officer. The customer owned a new custom designed and personalized named post. This enterprise paid for Nick's expensive tuition, and he only dug one post hole — one!

Age and physical difficulties that required surgery at the Cleveland Clinic forced me to close my life's chapter on digging holes and falling in ditches. My personalized service and attention to detail with customers was my trademark. When their check for my services arrived in my mail, usually a nice thank you note was enclosed. The professionalism and manner in which I practiced provided an unexpected long term reward — the acquisition of special friendships! It's delightful to be honored by customers who today continue to extend invitations to their Thanksgiving meals. In passing, they may wave and shout "we're having a cookout this weekend, you're welcome to join," or, "stop by during Christmas and come see us." Of course, I check their mailbox before I knock on their door to see if it needs "tuning."

Before I closed this business, Nicholas had graduated from Le Cordon Bleu and was a sous-chef in Miami Beach. His tuition was paid off. I now have an extended family of Nick & Dad's customers scattered about the city. I have proud moments driving down streets near Stratford Hills and Oxford and count four or five mailboxes in one block that I had installed over the years. They stand straight and are nicely painted with a ring of blue three-quarter gravel around their bases. I said to a homeowner-customer once, "Do not beat the paint off my post with your weedwacker!" The color, satin black, was the most popular for painting the posts. You thought white, I bet. The customer who picked the design and color, and who was my contact person, then wrote the check, was most often the wife!

Please keep in mind that during this time frame, I continued to focus on matters relating to my dominoes. They slowly were being toppled, but the overall objective still required work to be done. New medical complications of valve slippage with my internal Koch pouch had altered the norm and it also had restricted me to limited activities. Virtually everything I was involved in daily had stopped. I was going to need surgery — how soon — and at what hospital, were questions before me. My surgical procedure at MCV in 1980 was rare, and their first. This procedure to realign my pouch valve would require a specialist surgeon, and none were in Richmond.

In the fall of 2014, my spirit around Thanksgiving and Christmas had diminished. While most were doing seasonal shopping, Dr. Crawford Smith, a noted surgeon here, had referred me to Cleveland Clinic for a preliminary pouch examination. Doctors in Cleveland examined me and recommended surgery, as soon as I could make arrangements.

This major abdominal-intestinal surgery was different from my first two. It was different in three ways — I was 35 years older, hundreds of miles from home, and I no longer was married to a registered nurse. None of this concerned me. My age was fine, the Cleveland

Clinic is one of America's best, specializing in Koch pouch procedures, and there was my friend, "Di."

New Year's Eve was 24 hours away as I rode shotgun. Ms. Diana Birchak was wheeling my new Camry through Charleston, West Virginia, as we headed back to Cleveland. I was scheduled for surgery on January the 2nd. Nicholas flew up from Miami on New Year's Day. The next morning they prepped me for surgery. My son was understandability anxious as I placed my necklace and gold cross around his neck before they took me away to the operating room. They both hugged me, giving me support and expressions of love. I was about to go under the knife once more.

Hours later, I awoke in a recovery room. Di was at my bedside. Nick hadn't slept during the night and was nearby asleep on a sofa. Di had a measured smile and a mixed expression between happiness and uncertainty. I sensed something was different. This prompted me to slowly slide my hand under my gown, — it was gone! My hand touched a vinyl bag attached to my side. The surgeons found it necessary to remove my Koch pouch. They found Crohn's disease inside and upward into the ileum. Research data gives the average life span of a Koch pouch as fourteen years. My pouch had served me faithfully for thirty-three!

Nick flew back South after seeing I was doing well. Di remained nearby at The Tudor Arms Hotel. She visited me daily and enjoyed cruising around nearby at her old Alma mater, Case Western Reserve University. The change from inserting a tube to wearing and emptying a reservoir bag was a difficult adaption.

Living alone, with all of my family miles away, was more intimidating than having surgery. I had no one to help me except one loyal and priceless friend — Di Birchak. We drove out of Cleveland on a January morning, with temperatures at 7 degrees above zero. Her kindness allowed me to reside at her home for three months. She saw to it that I ate properly, helped me regain my strength, and coordinated the scheduling of my home health ostomy care, twice weekly.

* * * * *

Early one May morning, four months later Richmond Police Chief Al Durham was at his home shaving. He received a cell phone call from Sgt. Carol Adams, informing the chief that she had just arrived at police headquarters and discovered an elderly, frail, white man with a cane, and wearing a suit sitting in a lawn chair on Grace Street. Oh! — and he had two dozen beautiful red roses in a towering vase. After questioning the gentleman, she continued to advise Chief Durham that the man said he was there to see him. The Chief loudly responded, "It's 7 a.m. Carol, and this white dude is waiting for me — with roses?" That old, frail, white dude — was me!

The day before, I witnessed a site that crushed my emotions. I stood in awe as it cut to my heart and simultaneously pissed me off to the highest. I was standing on sacred grounds, a place that was special to and a part of me. I was in the presence of a symbol of sacrifice, pain, and service, while the smell of urine choked my breath.

In Nina Abady Festival Park, two blocks from City Hall, stood the Richmond Police Officers Memorial, abandoned, neglected and abused. It was badly obscured, towering up through bushes, weeds, and into tree limbs. The homeless had made a path around its base and were urinating behind it daily. This beautiful ten-foot bronze statue depicting a Richmond police officer holding a little lost girl, not only was forgotten — it was violated.

These past two days were during National Police Week. No wreath had been laid at our memorial, not even a bouquet of flowers. That evening, I had a florist select the best 24 roses he had. I started crying when I told him where I was taking them. Later that night, I got my suit ready, picked out my favorite tie, and went to bed. I got up the next morning at daylight, with intentions to make damn sure somebody placed roses at that memorial— today! Later that morning, Chief Durham was escorted to our memorial. He honored my wishes, placing the roses on the granite base. He had not been made aware that this police memorial existed.

Within hours after I held a press conference detesting this situation, city crews immediately began cleaning up the site. Everybody from City Hall to the police department, the Police Memorial Foundation, and the public were accountable for allowing this to happen. I patrolled the streets with nine fallen officers listed on the plaque. The most egregious disregard for honor and respect were from our active and retired Richmond police officers — still living!

In June, I selected a five-member committee with specific objectives — find a suitable relocation site for our police memorial – raise money to move it — and

move it! The first member that I felt was essential on
this committee was Chief Durham. He wholeheartedly
accepted. In addition was H. Penn Burke, the grandson
of a slain police sergeant who was killed in 1925, Tom
Silvestri, President and Publisher of *Richmond Times-
Dispatch*, and Stephen Bonadies, Senior Deputy Director
for Conservation and Collections, Virginia Museum of
Fine Arts.

Several attempts had been made to relocate this
statue over the previous twenty years. Our Richmond
Police Memorial Research & Relocation Committee
held a public relocation ceremony inside of William
Byrd Park, fifteen months after our first meeting. The
necessary money was collected. City council members,
the city administration, along with our Mayor Dwight
C. Jones, and the public were supportive of our cause.
On October 22, 2016, Virginia's First Lady Dorothy
McAuliffe, per my invitation, laid a beautiful wreath
honoring our fallen officers and celebrating our statue's
new home. It was truly a milestone moment. Police
Memorial sculptor Maria Kirby-Smith and Lynda
Solansky, her sculptor's consultant, were disheartened
to learn that her masterpiece had been degraded over
the previous years. They traveled here from South
Carolina and spent days waxing and restoring the luster
to the bronze surface. They also attended the ceremony
and were joyous of all the collective efforts to give her
art a new revealing. Our team of individuals gave this
memorial prominence again. We gave it a new home with
morning sunshine rising upon its face — we gave it a
new day!

A personal moment of respect, validation, and
honor far beyond that of the statue ceremony, was

bestowed upon me that day. What Chief Durham did was unprecedented. Never before in the history of Richmond has a retired police officer worn his police uniform in public, especially after he had been retired for 31 years.

I had boldly claimed on previous occasions with Durham, "If I was twenty years younger, I would beg to come back and work for you." I advised him that I still had my uniform that I wore on my last day, and that I had intended to be buried in it. For decades my tailored uniform has remained hanging in my closet.

I wrote in a letter to Chief Durham, "You would give me no greater honor than to authorize me to wear my police uniform during the October 22nd Police Memorial Relocation Ceremony." He gave me that honor.

An hour before the ceremony, I arrived at the Memorial Plaza wearing new police shoes, a set of new badges, and the same uniform that Chief Duling allowed me to keep. Wearing my uniform once again gave me a resurgence of pride. I felt a closeness to the memorial and the fallen officers that I had worked with. Durham's professional courtesy in honoring my request helped erase some of the sadness I experienced years ago on my last day in this same uniform. His authorized badge still pinned on my shirt is a confirmation of our admiration for each other. Every beautiful moment that day made it feel like I had never retired.

* * * * *

This past year had been an unanticipated endeavor for me. The end results proved that any citizen can unite a few individuals and make things happen. It

wasn't my leadership that many wanted to acclaim.
It was our teamwork and focused objectives to get
something accomplished promptly. It could become our
legacy. Durham, Burke, Bonadies, and Silvestri built a
foundation for me to contribute something special for
the families of the fallen and for Richmond. Each of
them and our liaison team deserve my utmost respect and
appreciation.

When I thought I could possibly rest and restore
my aching knees from standing long hours in Byrd Park,
I learned this wasn't about to happen. My cell phone rang
and the caller advised me to pull over if I was driving.
It was Doris Ann Kane from the *Richmond Times-
Dispatch*, informing me I had been selected as one of
the honorees for Richmond's 2016 Person of the Year. I
knew a number of people had sent in their nomination for
me regarding my involvement with the statue relocation.
This was a bit too much for this Amherst County farm
boy.

Weeks later, I was invited down to the *Times-
Dispatch* to do a profile interview. Wearing a nice
suit, I returned back there to do a studio modeling for
photographer Alexa Welch Edlund, who instructed
me to say "peaches" as her camera clicked repeatedly.
Different, yes — fun, absolutely! Sometimes, I take the
Times-Dispatch "family" peaches during the summer.

The annual luncheon naming Richmond's Person
of the Year is a unique event where the air is filled with
anticipation. Many of the metropolitan movers and
shakers are in attendance. It's kind of a "who's who"
gathering with great food, greetings, handshakes, and
politics. Mayor-elect Levar Stoney had just celebrated
a victorious mayoral election. His name drew instant

applause when he was proclaimed to be 2016's Person of the Year. I felt special and honored to be named a co-honoree with him and others listed, who were recognized as respected community servants.

During the memorial paver project, my left knee kept reminding me that it wasn't happy with my excessive activity. X-rays confirmed cartilage damage and images of bone on bone. I rode this out until I finished the relocation project, causing further stress and pain. In June of 2018, Dr. Gregory Golladay performed a knee replacement at the VCU Health Center. Again, the medical procedures prevented me going to my home without authorized nursing assistance. My faithful ally, Ms. Birchak, modified her residence, allowing me to recover on her first floor. I remained there for weeks until all medical improvements were accomplished and physical therapy was completed. I felt privileged and appreciative of her hospitality and support. Dr.Golladay's surgical qualities rank him as one of Richmond's top orthopedic surgeons. My replacement knee serves me well.

* * * * *

One hot, humid day in August, a retired Richmond police officer pulled up while we were laying the pavers around the statue. Janice Smith, who had recently retired from the department's field services, stopped by to visit for two reasons -– one to bring the crew cold bottles of water, and second to share with me her suggestion. The new location of our police memorial plaza was near an entrance to Byrd Park, at the intersection of Blanton Avenue and Trafford Road.

She walked up, smiling, and said, "Hey Burley —
you know what would be nice? To rename Trafford Road
Police Memorial Way"

"That's an excellent idea, I'll look into it," I
replied.

After the relocation ceremony, our committee
voted to support her suggestion. I immediately drafted
a resolution to have the road name changed and hand
delivered it to City Hall. The only structure on this road
is the city owned Trafford Pump House. We wanted to
respect the Trafford family and hopefully receive their
blessings. No members were located after an extensive
research.

Months later, I met with Mayor Levar M. Stoney,
and the City's CAO, Ms. Selena Cuffee-Glenn, and
obtained their endorsements to present a resolution before
members of the City Council. Once all of the required
procedures were complete, Mayor Stoney sponsored my
resolution. I spoke before City Council during its regular
meeting and council members unanimously approved our
paper.

Severe storms and scheduling conflicts had
delayed unveiling the new signs for more than a year.
Finally, during National Police Week in May 2019, a silk,
thin-blue-line flag was draped over the specially designed
blue street sign with white lettering. Ropes with silk
tassels hung from the flag, awaiting a tug from the Mayor
and Richmond's Interim Police Chief William Smith.

I led off the ceremony speaking of our
Committee's appreciation for City Council and the City's
administration to give our Richmond law enforcement

family this honor. In recent years, the last two officers who were killed separately in our city were Virginia State Troopers. I turned and directed my comments to State Police Major Steve Chumley, advising him to inform these troopers grieving families that I hereby proclaim, "That this street, *Police Memorial Way*, is their street too!"

After the Mayor's brief comments, we all walked toward the sign post. My intentions were for Stoney and Smith to each tug a tassel. Chief Smith graciously yielded and gestured that I join in with the Mayor. Our hands were high as we jerked the flag away. This solemn yet joyous moment made this whole project come full circle. Retired officer Smith's suggestion became a reality. We have funds remaining from the relocation project and I hope we can give additional honor to the two troopers. There are pending plans to meet State Police Superintendent Gary Settle and Major Chumley this spring to propose my plans to install two additional benches at the memorial plaza. Each bench will display a trooper's name on a bronze plaque.

* * * * *

Nine days later, after the street sign unveiling, I experienced a life-long awaited moment with heightened emotions of happiness. No, it wasn't like the emotion of happiness experienced when getting married. It wasn't like seeing my daughter graduate from Lynchburg University, and it was nothing compared to winning a lottery. It was an emotion never experienced. The moment overwhelmed me with elation, so much so that crying and trembling ruled the moment.

Sixty years ago, I made a mistake and quit high school. I carried a void of failure in my heart throughout the same period of sixty years. On May 24, 2019, that failure was forgiven as I marched with the 2019 Commencement Class of Amherst County High School. I proudly walked alongside the seniors as we entered center stage at Liberty University's Vines Center. Thousands were applauding us as we made our way to our seats. It was surreal. My white hair contrasting with the burgundy cap and gown with tassels harassing my mustache. It was indeed a new day!

There I stood. All the graduates before me were seated. My name was called — a pause — then a proclamation was read, acknowledging my military and law enforcement service and my contributions to society. The proclamation continued to say that I had completed the requirements for graduation from Amherst County High. As I walked past Superintendent Dr. Robert Arnold with my official diploma in hand, School Board Chairman Michael Henderson descended from the stage and embraced me. This was more than deserving.

I knew that my amazing and supportive daughter Dorrie and her best friend Lisa Mitchell were in attendance. Di was in Ohio attending her granddaughter's graduation. Nick remained in Miami. My sons Douglas and Donald made no plans to attend.

As I turned to walk away from Mr. Henderson, someone shouted loudly,

"Glenwood, you're the man!" I froze — emotions of validation buckled my knees. That voice was that of retired police chief Alfred Durham. I couldn't get to him! He and Di had snookered me! She knew he planned to attend, but I didn't. The chief had driven down from New York, picked up his wife Monica in Upper Marlboro, Maryland then they traveled to Lynchburg to attend this ceremony together.

It meant so much to me to hold my diploma and to hear Durham shout from the bleachers, knowing he and his wife traveled so far to witness this unprecedented acclamation! I impatiently maneuvered my way towards their location to embrace them. Dorrie and Lisa were tracking my white hair so they quickly joined us.

To witness Dorrie's pride was so beautiful to my eyes. Graduates and parents walked up and expressed their congratulations to me.

I purchased a school class ring in my Junior year, but never felt justified to publically wear it. I had it in my pocket, intending to ask Dr. Arnold, if he would he place it on my finger after graduation. Instead, I preferred to ask my inspirational friend Al Durham to honor my wishes. He did!

I traveled to Amherst in the fall of 2018 to speak before the County School Board. The public speaker's segment was restricted to County residents only. Being a native of Amherst and attending Amherst schools decades earlier, the district superintendent extended a professional courtesy, allowing me to speak. I expressed my lifelong, self-caused void that continued to impact my self worth, and failed judgment to the sitting members. I presented to them a formal request that each member review my history and make judgment if I was worthy of receiving an honorary High School diploma. Shortly thereafter, I mailed each board member and school administrators a half-inch thick dossier of my lifelong resume and professional profile. The board accepted recommendations from the school administration during their January meeting and determined I was worthy of receiving an official diploma.

I am currently leading an effort to get our Richmond Police Mounted Officers a new Equestrian Center. Similar to the Police Memorial Committee, I formed a Richmond Regional Mounted Police & Stable Project Committee in the summer of 2017.The conditions of the current police stables are considered by many to be deplorable and unacceptable. It is reported that City officials condemned the facility about 17 years ago. The funds currently needed for new stables have been recently approved. The new site was selected and architect drawings were finalized. My proposal was to build a city-owned equestrian facility large enough to accommodate mounted horses for the Virginia Capital Police and the VCU Police Department. These agencies would like mounted units, but currently don't have stable facilities.

Every single endeavor I have undertaken during this "New Day" era has centered around one personal mantra --- believe in what I'm doing. I have had the great fortune of working with and selecting individuals that apply my same principles, to getting the job done. All who have worked with and for me make my accomplishments worthy of sharing.

Having character is considered by some to be like owning gold. Integrity is equally valued and wisdom develops in due time, as it's fed by failure and success. Retired Sheriff V. Stuart Cook, of Hanover County, Virginia and a fellow police officer has all three. Cook retired from Richmond as a Major and Deputy Police Chief then honorably served the citizens of Hanover.

I learned a long time ago that I am never too old to listen and never too old to seek advice. I visited Sheriff Cook in his office just before I announced my candidacy for Sheriff up in Amherst County.

My question to Cook: "Stuart, I'm heading to Amherst to run for Sheriff." — What advice do you have to give me?"

I started taking notes while he gave me his summary opinion of the key points —

"Be sincere, humble, listen, make eye contact, speak with confidence, and remain dignified."

What Cook told me next was unexpected.

"Should you get elected, there is one thing you must do — give back to your community."

I didn't win the election, but Sheriff Cook's advice continues to impact me, even to this day. In recent years, I have been financially blessed enough to provide assistance to Amherst folks in need. A $5000 donation was given in memory of my hero, Amherst Town Police Chief Bobby Mottley, to Amherst Cares for their food pantry program, which feeds underprivileged school children.

Giving back in itself is rewarding, but donating to respectful causes carries a special meaning when it's done, giving recognition to individuals who inspired me.

In 2018, I funded five $2000 scholarships that were awarded to exceptional seniors graduating from Amherst

County High School. Three scholarships were named in honor of my vocational shop teacher Harold H. Higgins, and two were in honor of Chief Mottley.

Dr. Robert Arnold has been the Amherst County's school superintendent for less than two years. He has impressed me with his encouragement for excellence and academic visions. With a very small budget for computers, the students were sinking in stagnated waters of technology. A start-up program for vocational skills helped implement a new "Television and Media Production Class." Their existing computers were ancient and inadequate. A $10,000 check was written and presented formally during a school board meeting for five new Apple iMac Computers with 27 inch monitors. The kids were ecstatic!

* * * * *

Water never was much a factor throughout my life. All I knew was small mountain springs of crisp, cold water for thirst and the narrow creeks running from them. I thought a Jon boat belonged to "John". I fished for native trout with a radio antenna on the Forks of Buffalo River. Johnny Houses in Burley Hollow were not built with shower stalls, so I don't recall taking showers until Army Basic training.

Well — welcome to the fun world, Mr. Burley! Di and I were extended an invitation by Vicki and "CL" Moore to join them on a two-week Caribbean cruise in the spring of 2017. I was experiencing constant knee pain and hesitated to accept, but they eventually persuaded me. We had put so much time and effort in making the Police Memorial project successful and we both were

absolutely exhausted. Vicki and "CL" reached out
with their kindness and it was a shared and beautiful
experience of resting and relaxation!

* * * * *

In May of 2020, an act of severe police brutality
occurred in Minneapolis, Minnesota when a police officer
pressed his knee against the neck of a citizen for more
than eight minutes, causing his death. This triggered
massive uprisings, including injuries, violence, looting,
destruction and burning of properties in cities throughout
the nation.

Days following the Minneapolis incident the
City of Richmond, Virginia experienced a historic
transformation. Many nights during the month of June,
throughout downtown and areas near Monument Avenue
there were protesters looting and blocking fire trucks that
were responding to numerous fires set by individuals.
Dozens of store front windows were smashed. Towering,
century old statues and their pedestals were defaced with
obscenities and hatred. Rioting crowds roped and yanked
down memorials and monuments that were decades old
landmarks gracing our parks, and neighborhoods.

Our Police Memorial Statue was vandalized eight
nights during a two week period. Glass jars of red paint
were tossed on the bronze chest, repeated coats of spray
paint, including chemicals seem to be the violators
continued tactic to deface our Memorial. Obscenities
marked the granite base and surrounding pavers. To
protect it from additional damage and potentially being
toppled over, we decided to move it to a safe location
inside a warehouse. We raised the needed $6000
for restoration. James Robertson, a sculptor, and a

preservation expert labored for more than two weeks stripping paints, sealing, and waxing the bronze back to its original luster.

Its beauty protected with blankets, plastic wrap and blue painters tape, the Memorial stands stoic, waiting for the proper time to return to Byrd Park and face the sunshine of a new day.

During this period of turmoil there were heightened tensions between the violent protesters and the city administration, including complaints of excessive force, or lack thereof by the Richmond Police Department. There was an emergency at our Mayor's doorstep: the need to restore calm tor our communities that were living a nightmare of fear for their lives and protection of their property. Many observers felt that our city mayor, members of city council, and public safety officials were in a tailspin. Something had to change – quickly!

Richmond Mayor, Levar Stoney announced the formation of a Task Force on Re-imaging Public Safety. To my surprise, he requested that I accept his appointment to serve on this team. It's a privilege and honor to join this group of great diversity, including professors, educators, activists, and community leaders. We have much to hash over. I intend to serve the Mayor and my City with integrity.

* * * * *

I close this chapter with wisdom that the beauty of life is acceptance and sharing. A gracious life is learning and forgiving. Some of my earlier years in life I ran with demons, reckless winds burning my face. There was Kentucky whiskey, Harley's, and Wellington boots, — and times when I didn't give a rat's ass. Yet somehow, and for some reason, God still protected me and he loved me. — I just didn't love myself.

This poor, innocent child living on a farm, shaded by the colorful ridges of Virginia mountains adapted to working the streets and watching a human, his throat slit, his blood swirling around my shoes as he bled to death on the sidewalk — are forever memories. God knew his purpose for me to live, serve and contribute. I can imagine my mother and father smiling down at me from heaven, "You done good Glen!" I'm blessed today with a renewed life and another chance to give, another chance to laugh, and if need be to cry, — and accept the precious gift of a smile.

I know and understand that at this very moment, throughout this world there are thousands of little children, prostitutes, addicts and veterans who are submersed in emptiness, despair, and hunger. Humans who have suffered much more than me, and painfully some have lost their way. I, too, realize that many will die in darkness.   So -- I am truly fortunate.

God,
My faith,
The Medical College of Virginia,
My surgeons,
My family,
and my friends. —

They gave me a new day!

Special Memories

I knew Christmas time was near when my mom would let me stay up with her late at night to crack walnuts. She kept a ball-peen hammer in a kitchen drawer exclusively for cracking various nuts. Black walnut trees were scattered throughout the mountains. We learned the tree locations early while we were kids. Once the walnuts fell after season maturity, we took a burlap bag to the woods and brought them home for additional curing. She had this big old rock, kind of flat on top that she placed on her lap. With this little hammer, she cracked walnuts to mix them in her seasonal fruit cakes and banana nut bread.

It was exciting to be her little helper. My role in this was using utensil picks to remove pieces of nut in the crevices of the hull. She prided herself in cracking a hull, keeping the nut intact. That was possible, yet not frequent. The extra highlight for me was hearing the radio. Mom enjoyed listening to a radio station, WCKY far away in Cincinnati, Ohio. I remember listening to radio announcer Wayne Raney from Wheeling, West Virginia playing country and western songs.

For a seven-year-old, this was big time excitement. I'm downstairs where it's warm, helping mom, and experiencing some precious bonding, with music! If there was the slightest movement toward picking up a sample and tasting it, I surely expected to get my little hand slapped — a smile, with my mom's formal "No!"

* * * * *

Virgie and David Burley were distant relatives, living in a distant hollow. Of all the Burleys in Amherst County, they were the least educated and struggled to survive. They owned a small log cabin on a rocky creek bank. Virgie and Dave were somewhat reclusive, neither being employed, and without children. They never owned a vehicle, and never owned milk cows or hogs. A visitor might spot a half-dozen chickens near an old shed, pecking for grit in their neglected yard.

I enjoyed visiting them especially during frigid weather. With their wood stove ablaze, the cabin with six foot ceilings was always cozy. When I visited them, I entered an unlocked screened porch and knocked on the kitchen door. It was important to announce myself when questioned of my identity as Virgie's hearing was impaired. If I calmly replied, "Glen" it was unlikely she heard me. She then would summon Dave.

"Who dat. Dave? — "Dave, who dat at the doe?"

Dave never said anything — he wouldn't open the door or inquire through the door who might be the visitor. Virgie kept repeating to Dave, "Who dat Dave?"

There was a leather strap on the outside of the door that you pulled to unhook the inside latch. The hole the door strap went through was about the diameter of a nickel. If someone failed to properly identify themselves, Dave quickly slid his 20 gauge shotgun barrel through that hole about 6 inches! I had two choices — speak loudly, or haul ass from there!

Virgie had a couple of things going for her. She was kind, humble and always put quality tasting meals on the table. Dave had a small garden that served their vegetable needs well. Virgie was the "cornbread queen," always using a "tad" of wild honey". When she baked cornbread, the wood stove oven carmelized the honey near the edges of the cast iron pan. The texture was moist but her tad of sweetness gave the flavor some pop!

I will always remember that shotgun barrel sliding through the hole, and including memories of their cozy home and my fun visits messing with them doing boyish pranks. The memory most special was Virgil making me cakes. Everyone living in the Sardis Church community who baked sweets knew little Glen had a sweet tooth. I always entered through the kitchen when visiting them. Sitting on a table stand was a silver-covered cake dish. I always picked up the lid to see if sweets were inside. Rarely it was empty — this time it was. I guess she saw the disappointment on my face. Months later I visited Virgie and Dave. Like always, I picked up the lid, and again, the cake dish was empty. This time it was Virgie who appeared saddened and disappointed. I wasn't old enough to detect any difficulties with this elderly couple, such as health issues or financial challenges. Later when I started to leave, Virgie leaned over to be face to face with me, sharing a smile. "You bring me eggs, some flour, and sugar and I'll make you a cake." I think I yelled, jumping up to touch the ceiling, "Oh boy!"

For approximately 5 years, from the age of seven to around 12, I perfected a ritual of gathering necessary ingredients to nurture my sweet tooth. This wasn't a weekly or monthly craving. Twice a year is my guess, maybe on a Saturday or while school was closed during the summer. Remember my mother frequently baked sweets, along with my aunts. I knew that whenever these times occurred it was an exciting day of anticipation and happiness!

I borrowed Mom's handmade cloth bag to carry everything. I packed the eggs directly from the henhouse in a little basket filled with sawdust from the woodpile. Mom handed me a plate from her cabinet and off I went. This walk was all uphill toward the mountain tree line to aunt Ruby's house. She furnished me with sugar or flour in a brown paper bag. With eggs and sugar, I'm on a roll now, climbing up to the mountain "homeplace" where my father was born and two more aunts live. If Ruby gave me sugar, then aunt Ora and Ruth would give me flour. In a couple of years I had become a successful scrounger of additional ingredients such as Crisco, vanilla extract, and cocoa powder.

With all my goodies in tow, I headed through a patch of woods and across several farming fields to Virgie's. If I was lucky and it was early in the day, she might immediately bake my cake. As I got older, my patience was more considerate and I would return later to pick it up. This round trip trek was over a mile. I have walked further for a coke and moon pie!

Her cakes were simple, with just two golden layers of batter and tasty icing. From her dingy, narrow kitchen Virgil crafted her culinary masterpieces with love, and tastefulness, with chocolate icing swirling in waves of perfection. I recall once, returning home, that my desire overwhelmed my patience. Her cake hadn't even cooled enough to cut. I stopped along the way, whipping out my pocket knife and hacked a piece — or two! Some times when returning home, I stopped by Aunt Ruby's and shared my cake with her. Sometimes she cut out a section for her and Uncle William, as their supper dessert. She occasionally poured us some chilled milk and we treated ourselves to Virgie's cake as we chatted.

Mom never owned a cake dish so she would suggest I leave my cake in the "big old room" where it was always cool. Cakes and pies seldom went into our refrigerator — possibly because they never lasted that long.

These childhood treks were much more than about sweets. They blessed me with a fulfillment of nurture by family members sharing kindness. Virgie and David Burley have long been deceased, but I think it's time for another trek. I think it's time to find their graves and leave some fresh flowers. Scampering from house to house, gathering all the goodies, including hugs and smiles, was my highlight of childhood excitement. They each gave of themselves — to reward me with happiness.

* * * * *

Boxes of .22 caliber bullets were stacked neatly in my bedroom drawer. Every time I saved thirty cents I took the first opportunity to go in the Western Auto store in town and buy another box of fifty bullets. This started around the age of ten.

Yes, at the age of ten! Buying ammunition at the hardware was no different from buying a bottle of coke and peanuts at Sardis Grocery. Rex Pixley, the store owner, knew I was stocking up to have plenty of bullets for target practice. At the same time Rex knew I was saving money to buy my first rifle. He helped me with my savings plan by placing a small can on a shelf behind his desk. When I gave him 50 cents to deposit, he matched it with 50 cents.   All of my older cousins and neighboring teenagers had rifles or shotguns for hunting. I was eager to gain the cultural status of being old enough to hunt. A state hunting license was required at the age of fifteen in order to hunt legally. However, none was needed if you hunted on your own property. I considered the adjoining mountains in the hollow as Burley owned. Game wardens had little interest in squirrel hunters.

Two years later, it's estimated I owned about thirty boxes of .22 shorts, and .22 longs. Man! That's 1500 rounds and I don't own a rifle yet. Before I turned thirteen, I fell in love with a Stevens Model 15-A .22 bolt-action, single shot. It taunted me for months on a display rack in the same store where I purchased the ammunition. I enjoyed going in the store and taking it off the rack to hold and practice aiming it. Its size was appealing to sportsmen as "boy's first rifle."

It's August the 4th, and now I'm thirteen. Everybody knew I was waiting patiently to get a green light on getting my first rifle. By now I had fired other rifles and a couple of 20 gauge shotguns. I don't know, but I suspect Rex ran this pending purchase approval by my parents. I don't remember any conversation or position of approval or denial from either of them. I would call it silent rites of passage toward maturity.

It was a Saturday. Dad and I were selling produce off the tailgate and the anticipation was high. Have I saved enough money? Is my Stevens' 15-A still on the display rack? Yes and yes! Unknowingly, Rex, earlier had ordered the exact same rifle. He wanted me to have one that had never been handled by customers. That day I proudly remember leaving the Western Auto Store, running down Main Street with my new rifle, and placing it on my dad's pickup seat. A long awaited dream had finally come true.

Throughout the summer I kept the rifle barrel hot, shooting hundreds of rounds perfecting my marksmanship. We set green peas on top of a board fence, and practiced picking them off at 50 yards without the bullets striking the wood. I practiced shooting off match heads from stick matches positioned on top of fence posts at 50 feet. We actually tried glancing match heads to ignite the match. By the time hunting season was open, I was ready. My focus was aiming at the squirrel's eye to instantly make the kill.

I may have been an excellent marksman at thirteen, but the squirrels were outsmarting me. I knew my rifle and they knew their woods! My trips to the mountain were becoming disheartening. Then my lucky day came. It was near dark as I descended the mountain when I spotted a squirrel jumping off the spring house roof. Seeing me, it ran up a tree and began barking at me, twitching its tail. With a skyline backdrop, it gave me a clear shot. The crack of the rifle shot echoed across the hollow. I got one!

I was shaking with excitement as I ran home with my first squirrel. Mom was gathering eggs as she heard me yelling her name. She helped me skin and dress my prize kill. "Oh no! — where's my rifle?" Mom assisted me with lighting the kerosene lantern and off I went, back to the mountains edge to retrieve my precious rifle. My excitement carried over past bedtime. I couldn't wait to brag at school the next day with breaking news. I proclaimed killing my first squirrel with my new rifle!

* * * * *

The Nation's largest catalog ordering company, Sears & Roebuck sponsored a program for 4-H Club members in Virginia. It was named the "Sears Pig Chain Program", designed to promote youth enterprise and pork production in rural communities. To participate, the 4-H member and parents entered into an agreement with the Amherst County Extension Agent.

The agreement was simple – I went to another farm where a 4-H member was already in the program, and picked out a six-week-old female piglet from its litter then brought it home. I cared for and fed this registered pig for months until it became a mature hog and was ready to breed. When it appeared my hog was coming in heat, Mr. "Irby Dick" Cash was notified. Mr. Cash was hired by Sears & Roebuck to keep a registered boar at his property. When a request was made, he loaded "Willie," this humongous male and delivered it to serve my virgin swine. Depending on her mood, she may accept him now and "Irby Dick" luckily makes one trip. Maybe not, and he returns later for Willie. A twelve-year-old kid raising pigs with "Irby Dick" and "Willie" — I can't make this up!

The day is near and excitement is building. My pregnant, black and white Hampshire is showing signs her little piglets are near birth. I cannot wait to get home from school. "Please wait — I want to be home when they are born." During suppertime, my dad said he thought tonight was the night. He had helped me prepare a horse stall for delivery. Protective rails were built along the walls to prevent the mother from mashing her newborn.

As bedtime beckoned, I ran down to the barn one last time to check. The expectant mother was lying down and breathing loud. This experience was all new, and I couldn't sleep — was she all right? Dad went to bed hours earlier, but Mom was still up. She observed my restlessness. She gave me permission to take a lantern and return to the barn. "Be careful with that lantern," she cautioned.

The hours seemed endless, as it was way past midnight. Perched in the hayloft above, I continued my vigil. I see one! — another, little tiny dudes about 7 inches long, exactly like their mom, black, with a white stripe across their shoulders. Wow! They kept popping out, staggering around seeking Mom's teats. Daylight was breaking and seven baby piglets were having their first breakfast. I blew out the lantern flame then ran home with the news.

"She's got seven" as I burst in the back door. Immediately I fetched a piece of paper and wrote down 15 seven times. That's $105, I thought, I'm going to be rich. I quickly washed up, went upstairs to get dressed for school then ate breakfast. Before the school bus arrived, I had to check on my sow and her babies. Wait — there are eight now!

The next seven weeks were wonderful and educational. These little animals were so small I could hold one in my hand. The litter soon became trouble makers. At the age of four weeks they began rooting up the yard and scouting out the garden. Mom stayed confined in the stall, while her little ones scampered about. Now, they were six weeks old and the "not so fun day "was here. One by one, they were caught and each received a pieced nose ring to prevent rooting. The male piglets got flipped upside down and were castrated by a neighboring Burley, using his razor-sharp pocket knife.

A 4-H County representative occasionally visited me to assure all care was being exercised and the birthing site met approval. One special visitor to my hog lot was a Sears official from Chicago. My last visitor came to get his pig — a new 4-H member arrived on a Saturday with his parents. I had mixed up some red clay mud, and smeared some on the white stripe to mark the females. The mother sow was already in her weaning stage, so the pigs had started eating a liquid feed mix from a small trough. We were at the barn, and all eight pigs were busy eating. The 4-H student pointed to his selection. We grabbed her by her hind legs and quickly slid her into a burlap bag, tied up the end, and off they went. Unexpectedly, after all the excitement was over, my dad handed me a receipt showing where he had purchased supplement sow mix. His silent look indicated reimbursement. My participation in the program had come full circle.

Now, the happy part. Little Glenwood was the sole owner of a registered Hampshire sow and her seven piglets. Dad took me to Hill Hardware to purchase a 4-x-4 ft. stove floor mat, a brush and a small can of paint. I went home and painted five words on the mat then nailed it to a tree on Rt. 60, at the entrance to the hollow.

It read, *"Pigs for Sale - See Glen."*

Peace Within

Funeral services are held daily and caskets are closed then covered with tons of dirt shortly thereafter. Inside are human hearts and souls forever trapped with inner turmoil, restlessness and emptiness. Their chapters in life describing betrayal, lack of self worth, and abusiveness to name a few, are never resolved; leaving many behind with eternal scars.

My father's death was devastating to me. I learned why years after his funeral. His hugs, simple affection, and tossing baseball didn't exist. When he died — I hurt! We had buckets of dysfunctional slush between us. Only God knows what scars rode in my dad's casket. We owe it to ourselves and those we cherish, to lie in repose embraced with acceptance, forgiveness, and the inner warmth of peace.

An unspoken sadness in America is that millions die and never know who they really were. They never found a focus to understand why and how they thought as they did. Inner-family communications in my parents' and grandparents' generations seemed nonexistence. Today, society is text-obsessed or jabbering to the extreme with flash floods of social media. It's beneficial to many, but what comes with the good, comes also the toxic social media of hatred, scorn, and free-falling negativeness. This modern era of communication is the seeding grounds of hostility. When this style of dialogue is common practice by the sender, it becomes the norm during direct discussions. It breeds collective discourse in our society and threatens peace and harmony.

Cities across America reel in pain with high records of murder and domestic assault. Churches, funeral homes, and graveyards absorb the resounding screams of anguish throughout. The higher the anguish and deeper the hurt, the louder the screams. The deceased, usually a male, is likely the culprit. Running the streets, they brag about how many bitches they knock up, the robberies they pull, and possibly murdering someone. There they lie in the casket, bearing no guilt, no acceptance for their actions of pain. They leave behind despair and take emptiness with them. These funeral services are disgusting and yes — very sad. Dripping tears of honor and respect, and silent sobs setting one free to the heavens are far more beautiful than the screams of disdain. God does not want you in heaven with your guts full of hatred and unresolved slush. Closure is the final path toward peace. Living a life of wind storms and choppy seas never calmed, even to death, leaves no peace within.

World peace is praised. It's preached and prayed for across the globe. It's proclaimed as the ultimate answer to all conflicts, slaughter, and sorrow. Yet we don't speak much about our personal inner peace. How we function within and with others seems less significant. Our human brain can easily become toxic and the heart dysfunctional with unresolved issues dancing in our memories of life. The foundation of our life is the nurturing with loving encouragement that everyone is special and one of God's children.

There is so very much for which I am thankful. Thirty-five years ago, the high noon in my life, blessings came upon me with the best of professional help and friendship support. I conquered all evils and met the challenges to get well. With determination day by day, month after month, and for years, God and I eventually proclaimed my inner peace. I prayed for it, worked for it, and with his grace and guidance — I have it.

My masculinity didn't vanish when I asked for forgiveness, and told someone I was sorry. My confidence wasn't compromised when I wept with the deepest emotions for my regrets and acceptance of my failures. Bullshit with machoism! Marines cry. Paratroopers and police officers cry. It's alright to cry! It took years, one by one, to topple my dominos, then toss them to the winds. My hurts, misdeeds, and the search to be loved came full circle with resolve. Confidence replaced my emptiness. Genuine smiles and congeniality vacated my concealment of inner darkness.

When you finish this chapter, close the book — then sit in silence. Scan across your memories of yesterday, seeking a time when something happened to or with someone that's still unresolved. Break those decades of silence and say you are sorry, asking for forgiveness. Likewise what's equally important — forgive yourself.

Go find that someone and make their day. Make it your day too, finding that peace and celebrating closure and goodness of your actions. Trust me, your shoulders will be lightened, and your days will be brighter. You have just given yourself a priceless gift of inner peace.

By the time I reached forty, the accumulation of dysfunctional traits had poisoned my soul. My first twenty years suffered from an absence of self esteem and a void of childhood silence. My second twenty were confronting my demons from the first twenty. Perched on my shoulders was a large guilt and regret basket, unbearably heavy from struggling through two failed marriages and battling illness. My heart became tainted with spontaneous anger. The more the accumulation, the more the anxiety, and thus the more it weighed upon my shoulders.

The objective in this life and beauty therein is to set yourself free. Live life and walk with weightlessness in your heart and upon your shoulders. Carrying grudges and smouldering issues creates nothing but negative energy. Nothing healthy grows from strained relationships, allowing hurts to linger in time.

The love and passion of your parents brought you into this world to be creative, to contribute, and love mankind. Respect your blessings of God's love, living your life to the fullest while giving back a part of you. Let the final closing of your casket or the sealing of your urn take you beyond, leaving peace with all that you touched in life.

Allow your death to have blue skies, a calm breeze, with memories by them of acceptance, forgiveness, and closure. In our death, let life be celebrated, our rooms of experience are forever locked in time. Let the heavens welcome us as we enter a new day, forever — and peace within.